HEAVENLY PEACE, MY ASS

HEAVENLY PEACE, MY ASS

WHEN HAPPILY EVER AFTER HAS OTHER PLANS

ARIC H. MORRISON

THIRSTY CAMEL
PUBLISHING

HEAVENLY PEACE MY ASS

When Happily Ever After Has Other Plans

Aric H. Morrison

Published by:

Thirsty Camel Publishing.

www.thirstycamelpublishing.com

ISBN: 978-1-958246-00-9

Library of Congress Control Number: 2022907591

DEDICATION

This book is respectfully dedicated to Mr. Pinckney from Laconia High School English class; without him, I may never have fully realized the ability to share these words around the globe.

"A true test of the human spirit is never on display more than at those moments when it feels like the world is against you."

Aric H. Morrison

CONTENTS

FOREWORD

Heavenly Peace, My Ass, by Aric H Morrison, is a powerful look into one man's journey as a series of adversities and hardships befall him at every imaginable turn. The first of the Stealing Home Series delves deeply into dark times, family tragedy, and incredible life insights.

I know about family tragedy and dark times firsthand. Don't we all, to some degree? Do any of us have a perfectly unblemished past and present? I work at an inner-city safety-net hospital as a pediatric emergency medicine physician in Boston, MA. To say I have seen and heard it all is an understatement until I was introduced to Aric's story.

Every child I have ever diagnosed with medical trauma is from the loveliest family. Despite all my teams' efforts, children who have died in my ER often come from the kindest parents. There is a parallel here between my work to this book. And personally, I have had my share of trauma with one of my child's scary struggles with mental health. Again, relatable to elements discussed within this one. It's unfair. So is Aric's story.

"Mind-blowing" is what comes to me when I consider this book.

I met Mr. Morrison several years ago and knew that there were demons within. He is a truly inspiring man with a tale that needed telling. While I thought I knew him more than most in his inner circle, this first book in the *Stealing Home Series* left me speechless and incredulous.

There was so much more to how things unfolded from circumstances in his childhood than I'd known. They have haunted him. And for Aric, there is such a strong sense of family woven intricately throughout this story.

And this is how it should be; family is everything. It is the heart and soul of our lives. What could be more important? I know for me, it is my children, beyond a doubt. They are the single most crucial beings in my life.

For Aric, family has been the center of his world. FATE, CIRCUMSTANCE, whatever you want to call it, altered the composition of his family at too young an age and forced him into unfamiliar roles.

He has been a father figure to his youngest siblings and was creating his own family when tragic blow after tragic blow battered him. After reading this book, I wanted to call him because this was like nothing I'd ever experienced.

This book is written with vivid imagery, insightful analogies, family, baseball, and music woven throughout. While it is at times very dark, it has its moments of levity that had me laughing out loud (a feat not easily attained).

The writing is suspenseful and gripping. While I knew much of the story, I had no idea the depth of the emotional turmoil he suffered. I hurriedly read page after page, wanting to know what was next? I thought it could not get any more heartbreaking, yet it did.

No one person should endure such a constant progression of adversities. No one person should be subject to trauma of this degree like Aric. Throughout many of the chapters, there are heartfelt, redeeming messages that enlighten us about the important things in life.

He demonstrates the need for all of us to take time to live in the moment and recognize what we *have* and not dwell on what we *want*.

This journey will open your eyes to life's cruel hardships but will leave you with a sense of compassion, empathy, and hope. While demons haunt us all to some degree, it is what we do to overcome, conquer, and share a message of rejuvenation.

I have heard him on stage a thousand times speak in riddles about much in his life. I never knew, until now!

Aric so eloquently presents it all here finally, after years and years of contemplation.

He said in a recent interview, "It is time."

And after reading this first book, I am so glad this series is finally seeing the light of day. I agree with him. IT IS TIME.

What an absolute masterpiece.

Heavenly Peace, My Ass is a compelling first book that will leave the reader wanting to know what happens next. It will be brutal, almost torturous, to wait for the second book.

Barbara M Walsh, MD
Clinical Associate Professor of Pediatrics
Division of Pediatric Emergency Medicine
Director, Pediatric Emergency Medicine In situ and Mobile
Outreach Simulation
Associate Clinical Director of Pediatrics | Solomont Simulation
Center
Boston University School of Medicine
Boston Medical Center
Boston, MA 02118
781 382 8544

PREFACE

This endeavor began alongside the hospital bed of my ailing child. It has morphed into over eighteen different versions, rewritten countless times, as the aggregate word totals now exceed well over one million.

There were occasions when I was ready to leave it forever and consider it a cathartic experience meant just for me. And then, through introspection, determination, and song lyrics, I found renewed energy to continue.

The highly personal details within this book series are not meant to garner sympathy, pity, or special consideration. With experiences come lessons, and with those come ways to heal and inspire others hopefully. This book is a way to step out of your world to learn.

The reader is encouraged to forge through the winds of adversity and always be mindful to keep appropriately balanced no matter how difficult the battle is.

This book is a tale about a child introduced to many hidden, unpredictable circumstances. An accurate recounting that swiftly offers an endless series of disturbing events that seemed to arrive in succession with little room to process.

The chapters continued herein share the details of a poignant ride. Though some may be without much color, the theme here is to understand the many unpredictabilities we encounter along the way during this incredible gift of life.

I've done my job if someone reading this work can become strengthened from my lessons, dynamic errors made, incorrect assumptions, and overall pearls of wisdom.

And if these written pages can offer up some faint glimmer to those who are downtrodden, this fourteen-year project was certainly worth the effort it has taken me to see it through.

This, by far, is my most ambitious undertaking. It took a toll on me to constantly reopen my deeper wounds through the years. What is written here in this first book represents an introduction and then goes forward to serve as a backdrop for the others.

If books about rainbows and fluffy clouds are your thing, this one is probably not a good fit.

The themes contained here are deeply meaningful. This book serves as a reference to always be mindful about falling forward when struggling. It is all presented in complete detail exactly as it happened.

It would be foolish to believe much of the unrest I have carried with me cannot be blamed upon many of these early experiences presented in this book.

Here, I share my life.

We all have a story.

This is mine.

STEALING HOME

SERIES OPEN

START

M y lungs expanded with irregularity as each breath became a bit more deliberate. Standing on the infield on a warm, sunny day in August a few years ago, I sought what I had believed would be some form of finality by my being there. Many people had questioned why I was going to do this event in the first place, citing that it might be too difficult to get through. I didn't initially see it the same way, but more than a few reflective hours were had before I made the final commitment. There was nothing small about what we were about to experience, that's for sure.

If there ever were a perfect afternoon for baseball, it can only be assumed that perhaps this one was meant to be. The sky was blue, warm with fresh air, and the crowds were steadily flowing into their seats with excitement. It was just another day for everyone else, but not for me.

The smell of baseball was most definitely all around. The chalk on the grass was a mere foot away from the edge of my sneakered toe. I gazed back several times to see people eagerly perched upon their molded plastic seats, which would, for the next several hours, become host to their memories. Oddly, I could *feel* them.

The first few rows of fans looked at me with envy as I stood there before them on the other side of the field box barrier on the baseball diamond itself. My stoic facial expression probably added to my noticeable presence there. Many of them were intrigued.

If they only knew.

I'm not sure I can fully explain all the emotions I had been troubled with. There were just so many, including a blend of sadness, joy, catharsis, independent spirit, triumph, unimaginable void, separation, and jarring pain. Each one of them was individually rioting in my head, seeking to be named the victor. Maybe there was even a lingering sense of guilt. I had been wrestling for years to understand why my life had turned out this way.

The vantage point from the third-base line just left of home plate was unbelievable. The opposing team played catch and warmed up not ten feet away. I was standing in a spot most people never had the chance to experience.

Glancing up at the many rows of baseball fans, I knew there was an expectation on their collective minds. This day was all about *them* in terms of memory creation. In my opinion, only a ballpark can make this happen; this one does it the best.

I paid a heavy toll. It wasn't worth it. Waiting anxiously on the field, not a person in the crowd had any idea who I was or why the heck I had been fortunate enough to be standing there. With confidence, I can say that many people were interested in what they needed to do to receive such an opportunity; the very same opportunity I had been hesitant to accept due to serrated imagery still within my skull.

Truthfully, I wouldn't have wished my circumstance upon anyone. The actual cost of being there was one without denomination. My story is definitive and still very much unwritten.

It is one that dramatically altered the course of my journey while also deeply affecting my opinions and outlook on this so-called lifecycle.

I had well planned for our attendance in advance. Two luxury suites behind home plate filled up with friends and family members, business associates, and maybe even a stranger or two. For those guests supporting us who couldn't be accommodated in the suites, there were an additional seventy-five tickets around the first and third base lines.

Looking at the size of the crowd on hand, the park must have been close to a near sell-out. The place was noticeably packed, thus raising my nerves a fair amount with each entry who plopped down in a seat to stare.

About ten minutes before game time, I removed my ball cap, placed it across my chest, and lifted my eyes to the sky. A simple moment captured on film, as I later became aware. Thankfully, my watery eyes were not visible to all those sitting close to me in the stands. They could only see the back of my jersey, and me looking up for some unknown reason to the clouds above, ever so briefly.

I'm sure they never thought twice about it, as this gesture seems all too common in sports these days. But my reasoning, in contrast to theirs, was utterly different and much more profound. It represented significance beyond just a simple gaze up to the heavens. It was much more. It was my way to make it known that our presence was not only just for us. We were there to represent many people, most we had never met.

As the ceremonies are all very well timed and scripted appropriately before a ballgame, my nerves manifested themselves even more beneath my skin as the pre-game events drew nearer and nearer to showtime. Regardless of the uneasiness, I knew the result of my being there would bring closure, and with it, hopefully, some form of inner peace.

I had circled this baseball experience on my calendar for quite some time. Due to recent personally traumatic dealings, I'd even backed out of it once in my apprehension. I kidded myself initially to think this day wasn't necessary before accepting the fact that it needed to occur.

As someone read the script I had so carefully written the week before, elements of our very personal story floated poignantly through the speakers around the stands. My life was voluntarily being exposed to all of those in attendance. It was beautifully represented in this environment, detail after detail, spoken slowly by the man behind the microphone.

Before our arrival, I was scared shitless deep down inside that no one would care about what they were hearing. People would continue to yell, talk, munch on popcorn, swear, spit, and insensitively guzzle their beer while callously making a ton of inconsiderate noise. I couldn't control their actions, but it concerned me nonetheless. We deserved those respectful minutes.

In short order, I knew my assumptions had been all wrong.

To my surprise, despite their impatience for the game to begin, people *were* definitely listening to our story. They gradually quieted as the words continued to echo throughout the ballpark while various details captivated them. It was almost as if they could relate in some way.

People were pausing in appreciation to hear the current sentence, the next sentence, and then the next. The excessive crowd noise quickly diminished to nothing more than a hush.

Holy Crap, I thought as my eyes swelled.

This moved me from anxious to astonished in forty-five seconds. It wasn't just a few who could appreciate our trials; validation was immediately upon me from thousands of other people.

Despite the discomfort the advanced planning had caused me, today was a chance to start again. Both a literal and symbolic opportunity to take those first steps toward finding my own internal peace if it was even possible.

I double tapped my back right pocket just before reaching down to grab my son's hand. I awaited the cue to proceed forward while inhaling hugely.

No longer was any more time available to wrestle with the possibility that terrible things don't happen to good people; I know for a fact they absolutely do.

One way or another, the events from the previous years were about to be laid to rest. It certainly had been time to do so; steady adversity had rained down upon me suddenly and repeatedly for more years than anyone should ever have to reckon with.

This was a day like any other for most; for me, it was all about facing the demons one last time. I knew the painful memories all had to become real again. It was part of the healing process before attempting to move on.

This odyssey needed to conclude somehow; if not, it most certainly would have taken everything from me. The ceremony was my most significant opportunity to finally move away from the darkness which had consumed me.

The date was August 22, 2015, and so it began in front of 37,000 people.

HEAVENLY PEACE, MY ASS

MY ASS

GAME #1

PREGAME

THOUGHT

T hough the primary telling of this series is to recount the events which happened over a particular time, it is essential to understand the backstory of this guy named Aric, who has been privileged to share it with you.

Often, our most meaningful impressions come and then go without fanfare or extended timing. It isn't always easy to determine their immediate motives. They must never be valued by length because some of these memorable brain drawings are over as quickly as they began. Consider their impact first, and then assign them a forever spot close to your heart in order of benefit to you.

It's funny how we hold on to specific memories as if they were some of the most influential moments in our lives. A few may prove to be, while others not so much. We never know how powerful a place they may occupy later down the road. Some can take clear form, fade over time, or provide the spark we need to continue moving forward during more trying periods.

Before attending my first Sox game in person as a kid, I used to lay on the floor in the living room enjoying game after game with my family during those hot summer days. We all joined together around the television set, watching baseball games during the seventies. It was a small living room with only one couch and one chair, but somehow, we five fit nicely.

Rick Burleson, Denny Doyle, Jerry Remy, Carlton Fisk, Dwight Evans, Jim Rice, Fred Lynn, and Carl Yastrzemski are vivid reminders of whom my idols were while growing up on Gale Avenue in that house.

I recall drinking milk through one of the various glasses we had in our kitchen, where an image of Carl Yastrzemski had been printed on the side of it. After looking at the unique spelling, I remember struggling with how to say his name, slowly pronouncing it as it wrapped around the edge of the glass.

You could purchase jelly and keep the container to drink from, as they had the players' images printed on the side. We had many of these glasses in our cabinets alongside the McDonald's ones we acquired for free with food items.

Although tickets for Red Sox games were readily available, for some reason, the opportunity for us to go as an entire family and enjoy one always seemed to prove elusive. So much so that we never did make it to a game together as a complete unit back then. I always wished we had.

There weren't many times had with us all together, so when we did have the rare occasion to make it happen, it always seemed to be that much more exciting. I can only think of a few events.

Today, the tickets for a Red Sox game are quite the commodity and much more sought after. In those days, it was not uncommon to be watching them play on TV and notice many empty seats available around the ballpark. It looked as though, once in there, you almost had your pick. Many sections appeared to be plentiful and in short demand — unfair!

With each of those empty seats, a memory was never realized. A young dream was potentially left unfulfilled in some subtle, poignant way.

It's kind of tragic. If you consider it in this manner, many childhood opportunities are squandered during each game when a seat remains unoccupied for a wishful kid to enjoy. The *empty seats at a ballpark* concept has taken on an entirely new perspective for me over time, but as a kid, it just sucked.

How could so many people not want to be there, and here I was, a simple boy wanting nothing more than a chance to do so?

It never seemed right to watch game after game from a musty, old couch or worn armchair when we could have been there live and in-person if we only had planned to grab a few tickets. It couldn't have been all that difficult.

There should *never* be an abundance of empty sections visible for any game. Show me an available spot for a child to take it all in; I will instantly show you ten dozen of them who would love the opportunity to escape in one of those seats for a few hours. One chance might be the only time ever they can do so.

It is odd to look at it so poignantly, but my opinion will not change. Because of my story and how it all unfolded, baseball has taken on an entirely purposeful new meaning for me. How I view it now doesn't alter my same belief from back then in a straightforward observation; all children should get a chance to sit at a ballgame with their parents and add an extraordinary page to their playbook. Even if only once, as I had done.

I will continuously justify my position on "empty seats" at ballgames in support of anyone who has ever lost a child and must live with the regret of never sharing the day.

DAY

My dad, one Saturday in 1977, was gifted a specific validation each parent strives to obtain. He delivered a forever memory to our hearts in Boston. He finally brought us to the ballpark and provided my brother and me with a special rite of passage every New England youth so eagerly deserves to attain.

I could never have known then, as my older brother and I sat with our father at this Red Sox game, the importance of that memorable day. It has since become the most defining experience I had with him. Thank God, somehow, it has continually remained dust-free since then. From the years 1979 to 2019, this one mainly gathered very little.

I view it as an absolute dream for any parent to be able to sit there flanked by their children at such an innocent time in their lives. He knew what he was doing that day. To know for a few hours, you represent the whole world to them in every sense of the word — hero.

While typing, it came to me; this entire episode was not just about our trip to see the home team — it was a flickering slice of opportunity. The day was so much more than just any other for a parent, as the loving bond with a child can be reinforced powerfully in togetherness if we make it happen. I understand all too well now.

A ballgame experience like this is one I knew must occur again someday if fortune brought me, children. It was never an option to do so; just a matter of how soon the opportunity took place after having them. Fenway Park was always on the shortlist regarding parental requirements. I so wanted to give them this day!

I don't recall the opposing team or the actual score of my first game. I remember just being amazed at all the activities around the park. My brother and I initially proceeded to take it all in from the outside perimeter. There was a magnificent whole new foreign world to behold.

Families were everywhere, parents and children walking hand in hand as they hurried across the streets and toward the entrances. Anticipatory glances abound as I saw the other kids walking by with the same expression on their faces — the one I must have had upon mine with all the makings of a perma-grim.

There was an immense joy just looking around, hearing the chatter, and being among other hardcore kids — those who, like me, were smiling from ear to ear with exuberance.

Unique electricity buzzed all around us; the day had finally come, and we were checking off that special box with Dad. I'm sure that it meant more to him than it did us, in a prophetic sort of way which I now can relate to.

The simplest things to a country kid were unique while enjoying this big city stuff; the smell of sausages, onions cooking outdoors on an open grill, the constant sound of program barkers, or being in the middle of so many people. The facility looked huge too.

Did the lights go high up into the clouds, or did I imagine it?

Everyone was filing into the same place at the same time for the same reason. Collectively, we were about to take things to the next level!

Once inside, the uncompromising feeling of finally seeing in person the very ballpark I had watched on television so many times previously was one of complete thrill and utter amazement. Both senses reveled together within my blonde-headed, skinny body, fueled on that day by hyperactivity and bouncy leg jitters.

If my skin could have made itself possible to leap out from within, it might have happened a few times. I couldn't contain my excitement; most spoken words consisted in the form of one long run-on sentence — childhood at its finest.

"Yes, I would like a bag of peanuts."

The scoreboard looked as I had remembered seeing it so many times on television, but it was so much more. It was all crystal clear in person, and the lights were just a tad brighter. They stood tall like grand soldiers watching over us all. And don't even get me started about the monster in left field!

Seeing the cut green grass below on the playing field was equally unique. It looked almost soft and velvety to the touch as I Imagined running barefoot around, enthusiastically examining every inch of it. I would have loved the chance to find out for myself if only it had been available.

My wide-open, ten-year-old hazel eyes wandered and darted all around the infield. I was briefly fixating on how they had created the crossing pattern on the grass and kept it looking so perfect without any traces of cut strands. These curiosities were far beyond my comprehension level; they blew my mind. This place was like nothing I had ever seen. Pure magic personified.

Truthfully, the seats were not even good. We sat many rows back in the right field, beyond the foul pole and far away from any aisle access. But on that day, it didn't matter, and time didn't matter. The world around me didn't even matter. What mattered to me most was that I was there to share a game, proudly sitting next to my dad and brother, writing a page or two in my childhood memory book.

Again, based on all those empty seats we had noticed during those other games that summer, *I* felt the lucky one to be sitting there. All three of us were, without any doubt!

We might as well have been at Walt Disney World for about two and a half hours. I enjoyed everything there was to find pleasure in about this place. Because it had taken so long in my young life to get there, the confidence to return anytime in the near future was nonexistent. I made the most of the day, like any other person there.

Unfortunately, joy was only permitted to dance uncontrollably within me for about four innings instead of the entire nine making up a complete game. As magical as it had been to allow every second of the game to soak in, it was also over abruptly as we gathered our things in what seemed out of the blue.

We left the game hurriedly as dad complained to us about having chest pains. With his history of cardiac trouble, there was always the possibility of arrest at any time. He knew the indicators and early warning symptoms all too well.

Instead of enjoying the wonder of it all entirely by remaining and seeing it end more traditionally, I sat in the front seat of his Mercury Cougar, white-knuckling the door handle for the majority of the ride, petrified he might be having another heart attack.

I prayed silently to myself for the whole two-hour drive. If he had one behind the wheel, it was game-over for the three of us.

I imagine how my poor dad must have felt to close our dream time so quickly like this. His sense of pride had to have suffered a blow; it could not have sat well within him to be at the mercy of his medical limitations. Once, we canceled a much-looked-forward-to vacation in Florida for the same reason. Oddly, we were used to it. Still, it wasn't any easier.

He tried his best, and in my mind now, he succeeded in his objective regardless of how short the day had run.

There are times we try our hardest to deliver on the promises we make to our children. Even then, some are made to be broken.

My young existence's highest and best day came crashing down in minutes. The trip was all gone; the spectacle was over, never to happen again with him. At the very least, my brother and I were able to have that one special day. Dad had created it.

What a twisted irony as it set the tone for the next forty years.

Circumstance had stepped in and taken away my fantasy. It beckoned me to push the day back into a folder of reflections deep within my preteen mind.

It was so disappointing to lose this one, but much about life cannot *really* be counted on, as I have since discovered.

FIRST INNING

BACK

As seventies kids growing up in New Hampshire, we initially were young hopefuls. We loved the game of baseball and everything about it. My friends and I often dreamt of having our names and pictures printed on the baseball cards we collected and traded. It was just a fun part of the process of being so wide-eyed and enthusiastic about such simple things. It was our world and our opportunity to imagine. Maybe the natural beauty of it was the possibility.

We lived solely to have fun, as any youth should be allowed to do. My childhood pals and I were all just crazy kids loving the game, Lake Winnipesaukee, and riding bikes down to Opechee Park for sports. A surprise candy bar from Mom or Dad and a quick trip to Dairy Queen or Weirs Beach made us happy back then. It was all too easy.

With many of my grade school friends from Pleasant Street, we yearned each time we played a baseball game to one day "make it." We had always figured at least one of us was going to. At eleven years old, it seemed more than likely. This possibility motivated us to play almost daily regardless of the weather. Hard or whiffle, it made no difference.

Back then, everything was obtainable. None of us ever wanted to hear that we might not attain any of our dreams. You lived them in your mind daily, they were all yours, and each one still had a probability of coming true. The only thing stopping them from eventually happening was our limited thoughts. It had nothing to do with skill at that age.

The odds of making it to the big leagues were quite astronomical, but we didn't care. Having grown up in Laconia, I was no different from any other in the country, sharing the same aspirations for fame. It was either baseball or rock star drumming to do it for me. I was always hopeful that one of them was going to come true. Youth is the only time your opinion can tell the world it is conquerable, and the mind still considers it so.

Paul Charles Caravello, aka "Eric Carr," from the famous rock group KISS became one of my absolute musical idols back in the day; I was sure if I made it big, my drumming style would emulate his. The music sounded like thunder. The guy rocked those skins and made a statement every time he played live in concert. I always imagined meeting him later on when I was older and sharing his influence on me.

My first ten years were undoubtedly some of the best, but you didn't realize it as a child. They are indeed the days of carefree innocence and wondrous possibility. As time has forced my maturation, I also understand that my early childhood was not necessarily representative of all kids. Good fortune doesn't unfold this way for many children.

Genuinely I wouldn't say I like knowing that somewhere else, another person could be writing about how smarting their memories of youth might be for them to recall. It would be nice to block out this truth, but tragically for some of them, childhood is anything *but* carefree. I never considered it decades earlier, but I certainly do now.

There aren't any days that pass without having my exposures through the years remind me of such. Everyone has a story; for some kids, theirs' begins and ends at a very young age.

Sadly, I saw it firsthand. My buddy committed suicide by hanging himself the day after Christmas.

I learned early on that our circumstances here can be unfair.

The taking of his own life always made me appreciate how lucky I had been to grow up in the environment I had. There were never any health issues and nothing to inhibit mobility.

To this day, I still wonder how terrible things must have been for my pal to take such action and end it all so early. It has never made any sense to me. When we played together, he always seemed like he was just one of us. His outward appearance implied his lack of financial resources, but none of us cared about that.

We hadn't known there was a torment hiding *inside* him either. He had been dealt a bad hand at home from a young age by being the offspring of an unstable mother. After he died, there were rumors, but nothing concrete was ever known about what had been going on. Not his fault at all. But in his head, leaving this world was the better option.

You never know what the actual picture is in another person's mind, let alone behind those mysterious closed doors we always refer to.

His passing opened my eyes to how complicated we all are when pretending to be in a place that isn't real.

I understand now, I did it for thirty years.

SALT

There was some powerful stuff I had been exposed to that had been less than ideal; my childhood wasn't all cotton candy and carnivals either.

I had become well versed in the acronyms ICU and EKG by the age of eleven. At Lakes Region General, my brother and I had the route memorized from the patient rooms to get to the snack machines and cafeteria for treats. We even used a microwave in there for the first time and thought it was just about the coolest thing ever!

I am sure it was not meant to scare us, but the continuous patter of heart attack threats took a toll on my psyche. It was ingrained in my still-developing mind that our father could have another one at any minute. Constantly looming, it was always hovering over our home. It was real because he had already suffered from them starting at age thirty-two.

We three (my older sister, older brother, and I) were expected to do all the chores around the house which required any degree of physical exertion. We raked, mowed, shoveled snow, stacked cordwood, took out the trash, did landscaping, gardening, moved furniture, and performed just about every other laborious task that needed completing. We were constantly doing things like this, so our dad didn't have to.

Imagine the heavy weight for a kid playing baseball in Little League, thinking that if he took the day off, causing his father to do physical work, it might trigger a heart event. I reminded myself that I was constantly busting my butt around the house to keep him alive.

The guilt would have been unbearable if something had happened to him after I put down my shovel or rake early in protest, and he then did the work.

That is a lot for a child.

There were days in third, fourth, fifth, sixth, and seventh grades that I can recall hearing the news from my mom and being taken away suddenly to stay with friends or family during those initial couple of days when things were serious.

After school, my brother and I were picked up and taken to the hospital for the remainder of the afternoon into the early evening to be with Dad. If there was homework, it was done in a hospital room. *This* was just what we did.

We were not even allowed to see him on some days because his condition had worsened. We then hoped to be able to visit him tomorrow.

One Christmas, we spent the eve with Dad in the hospital and opened our presents at home in the morning. Traditions were routinely broken like this as we drove back to the hospital to be together with him shortly after having some stocking candy and examining our gifts.

Medical facilities were quite familiar to me as we traveled to Boston weekend after weekend to visit my ailing grandfather for what seemed like a year.

The floors were lined with colors, making it easier to know where to go. I always thought it was quite fun to trace the lines with my sneaker as we followed them to find Grandpa Morrison's patient room.

He passed away in the hospital and never made it back home.

There was nothing conventional about many of those earlier years, that much is certain.

I also fought immense anxiety issues as a child, to the point that by fifth grade, I almost stayed back due to so many missed days. Monday after Monday after Monday I rode to elementary school, bawling on my bike because I dreaded walking into my classroom. The other four days of the week were acceptable because the environment was comfortable by then.

After taking the weekend off, the process started again on Monday morning. It was horrible worrying all weekend long and then waking up on those days and crying for two hours before class started. The school had provided a therapist sporadically, but it didn't help me.

That summer, I was sent to 4-H Camp for an entire week. After hearing from another person, it was a fantastic weekend away; I was all in. It became the worse decision I could have made. I cried myself to sleep each night after being paralyzed with anxiety all day long while being forced to participate in such a strange and unfamiliar place. There was rarely a sleepover to be had anywhere because I knew what would inevitably happen.

Participating in school sports was an absolute pass. I only made it through one basketball game in youth league because the crowd and gym atmosphere intimidated me so much. Baseball was the only sport that I could feel comfortable with because we played it, and it was familiar. I was very athletic and excelled in that sport. Of course, band was the other one that offered me confidence as there was a lot of talent within me.

I never understood why any of this happened, only how terrible it was to have this affliction. Not knowing it wasn't normal, I figured everyone behaved similarly. None of it was ever formally diagnosed until later when I started putting the pieces together independently. Today it all makes sense when I look at the patterns.

Now, I can be fine on a stage in front of a thousand people. I am in control because they are there to see and hear me speak. Over time too, you learn how to challenge that which affects you and become very strong.

And then there was the ADHD, a learning disability, a processing disorder, and body shaming, to round things out nicely. None of this was diagnosed either until decades later.

There was more. . . lurking within our four walls.

Some well-hidden family secrets resided in our house, which caused an entirely different level of instability for me above my other emotional frailties. I will share that this dynamic, too, contributed to additional nights when I cried myself to sleep.

I'm happy to still have two stuffed animals from my youth packed away, which somehow have survived. One is a black and white bear named Teddy; the other is a green dog missing one eye named Pillow. I loved those two; they were loyal.

I am unsure if they represent a good reflection or a bad one.

Both were soaked from my tears more times than I might like to consider.

GAME

*W*hat I speak about here was such a disturbing series of events for me that I have blocked most of it out completely. Only until I began writing this book had much of it come back.

As I continued to force the memories, more painful details resurfaced in my mind. It may have been better to let these remain dormant like some of the other ones mentioned previously. After pondering for quite some time, these two chapters were the last to be added to this book.

Remaining faithful to my purpose of writing and hoping to inspire others, I committed to myself when I introduced my life story to the world if I was going to share nearly everything; it meant just that, including what happened in the summer of 1979.

The term *grooming* seems all too prevalent these days as more and more cases of children becoming prey to sexual predators are discovered. I hadn't fully understood the magnitude of this series of events at the time, as I, too, fell victim to one of these pedophile bastards earlier on in my years.

At one of the churches where we all attended, I was an altar boy for the 10:00 a.m. service on Sundays. Truthfully, we were not an overly religious family, but we attended our fair share of services through the years. Enough for me to feel comfortable giving back in this capacity. I attended Sunday school there when I was very young, so it also seemed appropriate in some small way.

There was an ulterior motive in my doing so as well, her name was "Kerri", and I had one hell of a crush on her. She, too, worked the same job as me, and I got to see her there outside of our middle school encounters. Sundays with Kerri became a huge bonus to be around her and melt a little.

A man approached me after one of the services to inquire if there was any interest in my babysitting their two children. Because they were a part of the parish, and I knew them, it didn't require much convincing to agree. When someone familiar offers a chance to make money at a young age, you take it. I saw them every Sunday sitting towards the front of the alter close to me; they were trustworthy.

Most of the babysitting was occasionally on Friday or Saturday evenings while attending shows at a local playhouse in Gilford. I probably made around five or six bucks for this task, but it was good money. All I had to do was play with the kids for a couple of hours, and as much junk food I could eat during that time was also provided! It was a dream come true for a first job.

I babysat between twelve and fifteen times that summer and into the fall, which was *more* than enough. The father of this family of four hadn't taken long to introduce his plan.

First, he always went out of his way to step up and let his wife know *he* would be the one who drove me home. Not once had she ever been allowed to give me a lift. It was **always** him. Even when I insisted on walking, it was never an option. This pattern alone should have been my first indicator that something was amiss. Being a young boy, I never gave it any mind.

The true weirdness began on our second ride with casual conversations about my siblings and his wanting to inquire if I had seen any of them naked recently. He wanted to know if I had any questions about other nude bodies I may have noticed while hanging around with my friends, in the locker room for gym class, magazines, or movies. More so on the male side and less on the female end of things. He was always strangely overeager to hear my answers to any of his questions.

After a few more rides home with him, it became clear how focused he was on learning more about *me* specifically. This man always wanted to know how much I had learned about the physiological changes in boys and girls around my age. I understand now that he was calculating potential puberty and body changes for the kid sitting next to him in the passenger seat.

He must have regularly targeted a particular age range to become his sexual prey. Unquestionably it turned him on to consider me undergoing these standard progressions. To think he was the parent of a little boy and a little girl.

On another occasion, the conversation continued with his curiosity about the existence and color of any pubic hair growth. Again, it was very uncomfortable to talk about. Still, there was no big picture concern alerting me to run away from this filthy piece of garbage, so I willingly shared my personal information with him. I fed his appetite.

On one drive home, he focused entirely on my sexual preferences leading to whether or not I had any girlfriends. He was trying to find out if I was gay. Probably in his vulgar fetish-laden mind, he was hoping I might be attracted to him? He was a married man, so it never registered that he was something other than heterosexual and seeking out young boys my age.

He was a homosexual and a very disturbed child molester. Apparently, he was in the market for some new innocent bodies. I fit the bill nicely for him.

I still didn't understand or give much thought to this stuff but knew I dreaded those rides after working in their house. It was just a matter of time before leaving their place to drive me home that he transformed into "creepy-leering guy" shortly after starting the engine. It was around thirty seconds before his mind engaged in sexual thought and flowed freely through his yellow teeth-stained mouth.

I shared my preference for girls regularly and even spoke fondly about the one I was attracted to from school and church. It seemed harmless to do so as I enjoyed talking about Kerri because there was such intrigue in her.

Unlike him to listen and then change the topic to sports or something else, he immediately wanted to know if I got an erection while dancing close with her at a recent mixer event. He then spent the remainder of the drive home telling me how easily he would get them at my age and still does.

How was I supposed to respond to this? I was just a kid trying to make a few bucks.

Nasty, auburn-haired, glasses-wearing, skinny, perverted, "family man" guy always made it a point to assure me it was ok to discuss these sexual things with him. He knew, "I must have had questions." This statement always led to his new agenda item for the current ride. As if he were some sort of trusted resource that I should feel comfortable confiding in.

It was odd to have this kind of conversation all the time, but being so naïve, I walked right into his world and kept tossing logs on his miserable warped fire, week after week. I wouldn't say I liked answering him when he probed me, but I always did so due to the respect for adults instilled in me. After all, he was also a member of my church.

Each ride home became increasingly problematic as his sexual topics involved more and more graphic details. This cretin became so obsessed with my presence that he even went out of the usual route to drive me home by taking the longest one possible to continue on his path of enjoying me for just a few more extra precious minutes of sickening conversation.

Week after week, I sat there.

On one humiliating trip, he presented me with a pornographic magazine and insisted I look at the pictures with him to "prove I was attracted to girls."

Again, "it was just a game".

Why was I allowing this man to treat me like this? This father of two young kids was an extremely sick individual.

One of the worst I ever took with this man turned very scary when he became insistent on discussing wet dreams and masturbation. He made assurances that I understood it was OK to do so. And then inquired if it had been something I might have considered partaking in with him the following week.

The abuser wanted me to share my thoughts about this and "probably was going to request" I watch him do it during most of the car rides, very soon after.

He even "educated" me as to how warm it was to the touch when his "fun" eventually came shooting out from doing so.

A really lovely, wholesome conversation to have with an emotionally frail young lad who dreamt of ballparks and playing music in arenas when he grew up.

The same boy who walked to movie matinees on Saturday and once a circus to do the things a child his age was *supposed* to be doing. Always sitting alone to quell his anxiety and hide from a few of the more difficult exposures that had haunted him at home so regularly.

Three precious hours to enjoy innocence by watching cartoons with a smile before the shows, eating candy, and escaping from routinely bad adult things.

There I was, facing an entirely new reality each week in the front seat, now processing *even more* bad things.

A grown man was one step away from taking his pants down and fondling himself in front of me.

Or even worse.

Note:

The most important lesson here is to let people know, EVERY child is at risk. This event was all on me, I kept it in.

Ask questions, watch behaviors, and allow for open communication with your children. I hold myself accountable for not speaking up early on.

DIRT

Pedophiles continue to feed their sexual appetite by taking larger bites of the child molestation apple. With each clamp down, they feel a trust to take more. And this is how it continues.

They have no regard for the damage they are doing to young impressionable minds; selfishly, they want to pleasure themselves all for the sake of the thrill.

Weekly, I was in a closed space with a man who I thought initially had good intentions by having me babysit his kids. Only to discover that I was becoming more and more entwined in his spiderweb of filth.

A Saturday evening in October, before one of my last babysitting occasions, the piggy man reached over confidently. He placed his bony nicotine-stained fingers on my upper leg during the ride home. I have no recollection of what the conversation had been about but knew this was inappropriate for sure.

Should I act as though it wasn't any big deal?

Do I move his hand away?

What if he got mad at me for bringing it up?

Was this going to lead to him touching my genitals?

I did nothing but sit there, frozen.

He selected an extra-long way to drive me home that Saturday.

Still, I told no one.

I sat there paralyzed the following week again, not knowing what to do. This time he started on the top of my thigh and slowly moved it over to the inner region of my leg. He guided his boney digits back and forth for a few minutes before taking his next bold move over into my inner thigh.

I could hear the sound of his breathing increase as he was performing this invasion of my own bodily space. He was in absolute hunter mode and was most definitely zeroing in on his next meal.

Who knows what this guy had in mind for the long term? His progression was evident that he had no intentions of ceasing his pursuit of me. As soon as the physical stuff was introduced, it would continue and lead to more aggressive behavior based on his previous history.

This was trouble; by then, I knew it.

He had crossed the line a few times in my mind, but I didn't stop him, still unsure if he might drive the car somewhere and hurt me had I attempted to.

I began to place myself in tactical strategy mode and knew if I could only appease him, I would be safe for another week to deal with it, and collect another check for babysitting.

Towards the end of these encounters, I was a mess getting out of his car and even felt personal shame walking to the safety of my house.

Eventually, a kid can only take so much. This physical and sexual abuse was not worth the money at all.

So just before my last babysitting job with that family, I worked out my exit strategy.

As it became unbearable, I set my plan in place for one final ride. The goal was to make him believe all was well and that he would see me again in seven days.

I played the game, knowing *this* would be the last time I ever would be trapped in his car.

Obediently I sat there and allowed him the pleasure to caress my leg and work his hand over to my crotch for seventeen agonizing minutes all the way home.

I was being sexually assaulted.

This behavior was a part of the sick thrill game he played with young people, routinely peeling open their innocence and using it for his masturbatory pleasure.

This person stripped me of my dignity and trust in adults. I know it impacted my lifetime ability to get close to others. I was the victim, but HE caused me to dislike myself immensely.

It bothers me how long I allowed him to stalk, manipulate and abuse me.

How many other innocent kids had been exposed to his mission? I live with the regret that I permitted this progressive behavior to continue for months on end without telling anyone or having the wherewithal to know what was going on.

Since writing these chapters, the recollection has profoundly shaken me. There is shame within for looking the other way while this man abused me repeatedly. It bothers me now that I even engaged in these interactions with him without understanding the larger picture.

I can still see this male sack of excrement smiling at me while peering through his glasses and lighting up one of his long, brown, skinny cigarettes before walking me out to his car.

He knew I was his captive audience for the next fifteen minutes. Therefore, he always grinned from ear to ear before sparking that thing up in celebration.

The smell of his stench remains deep within the back of my nasal passages. In his mind, I was property. He probably looked more forward to driving me home than the shows he and his wife attended on those Sat evenings. I hate to think about what he did after I left his vehicle.

Like so many unfortunate other children, my name can now be associated with the *victim* word. There is no bow to tie around this one to pretend all is well with what happened to me.

I live with it, deal with it, and regret it.

Undoubtedly, the summer and fall of 1979 shaped me to distrust, distance myself, and never want to get close to people.

The babysitting job gave me extra cash in my pocket to buy toys at the store or ice cream on a hot summer day. Not wanting to be a burden on my parents and ask for money for those things, I simply chose to pay my way.

Watching their children and then sitting in the passenger seat being subjected to this man seemed a way to earn a few bucks on a Saturday night, though it was a rough play.

Our kitchen had a substantial rotting hole in the ceiling above the table. The water came down through the roof and dripped into a well-placed bucket for collection when it rained. Pieces of the ceiling plaster, paint, and moisture-rot would continually drop down and dot the area when it wasn't raining. My young mind figured if there hadn't been money to fix that thing for a bit, there certainly wasn't money to toss at me. So, I earned it.

In this case . . . the hard way at age twelve.

Note:

Eventually, I did share with my mother a tad bit of information after I was done working for sicko man.

Because this pedophile was an active member of the parish and around children, mom reported him to the minister immediately.

She wasn't believed, and our church did nothing about it.

I am unsure now what was worse: the actual physical and psychological sexual abuse, or having my place of worship call me a liar.

I never went back.

SECOND INNING

PLASTIC

Imagine being able to work as a roadie putting on music events every Friday, Saturday, and Sunday. I was in heaven. The extra-long tan-colored van would pull up in front of the house, pick me up, and off we would go to put on another performance. Music, lights, fog, and a visual array are what we offered.

Dances, weddings, events, shows, we did them. I traveled all over New England and absolutely loved my weekends putting these on. Our boss "Rick" was a radio personality, so it was a perfect side hustle for him.

In contrast, after working for the touch and feel pervert a year prior, this was now the best job ever.

Together with the "guys," we became so efficient in our craft that when pressed, rarely did we not make the deadline to have music playing when the contracted time began. Talk about a well-oiled machine; we indeed *were* that. We knew our stuff like professionals; I could set that entire performance up from start to finish with my eyes closed.

My boss had regularly presented me with raises, and I was fortunate to learn much about audio and video technology and working a crowd. It was so cool to be in this unique space for a young person; obviously, it was cash under the table. I wasn't of legal working age but enjoyed making money, traveling, and being a part of the production. Oh, and yes, I met a lot of girls too!

As my friends were home on the weekends, I was out there learning a big person's game in show business.

Unfortunately, when you become a part of this lifestyle, there is also exposure to the ugly side of being on the road, in this case — cocaine.

In the eighties, it was pretty accessible and a routinely convenient means to make it through some long days. It was one of those habits I had been aware of but never exposed to until now.

Suddenly, there were large quantities in my proximity most of the time on these gigs. I was growing up fast around this sort of risk bubble. I knew the stuff was illegal but figured it was all safe to do what we did in terms of having it close to us.

What initially started as a small crutch became something much more significant in a relatively short amount of time. Rick was newly introduced to it, became hooked, and so began his downfall.

I know precisely when the dependence started for him and who the person was to get him addicted fully. I despised going to that dealer's facility for events because he was such a scumbag, and I resented him for what he had been doing to shake our stability.

We would set up, the bossman would disappear for fifteen minutes and then come back wholly a different person to begin the show. I observed this poor fellow becoming more and more of a servant to this nose candy, month after month.

It got so bad that we were transporting larger and larger quantities around in the van with us. It was hidden in a secret compartment in the mixing board, which we loaded for every job.

By the first six months into this work, I carried illegal drugs in and out of our show venues each time we set up and broke down.

I truly enjoyed that job and wasn't overly worried about us lugging white bags around. I wasn't doing cocaine, so I guess it hadn't mattered to me enough to consider what may have happened if the police had ever intervened.

It was almost as though I was living a double life, and none of my schoolmates had any idea. Nor did my parents. If I had told them, the job would certainly have been lost.

By the end of the first year, Rick was ultimately out of control on that stuff and experimenting with other substances. There is no way for me to know how much he was doing himself, but it was significant. I saw the packages.

He couldn't hide his use from us; we knew his routine. We heard him when he was off behind the curtain mid-song to snort a line or do a shot. His eyes gave him away as well.

After loading up our gear, he drove us back in that massive van while in a constant state of paranoia. He routinely assured us that "if we ever got pulled over, the police would never find it."

How comforting, even I knew where it was.

It was sad to watch him deteriorate so quickly. He was a family man with two young children, a beautiful home on the lake, and his life was spiraling out of control.

Is this really what grown-ups do? I wondered.

In July of 1981, things came to a head, and it all crashed down.

No longer was the job fun because the drugs had taken over entirely and become a new priority. What we were doing to please the crowds, satisfy contractual obligations, and make money all became a casualty of his new agenda.

He was a full-fledged cocaine addict. I believe he was also dealing during these appearances towards the end. Our show production business had become a front for his new illegal activities.

As addicts do, he got so messed up at the show one final night in July that he could barely drive the drug and cocaine-loaded van. I knew that there would not be a good outcome as soon as I had to help him into the driver's seat.

Thankfully it was very late in the evening with minimal traffic, so his nodding off and weaving from right to left on Interstate 93 North did not result in any crashes.

I had to reach over and grab the wheel a few times while waking him up. He was in no shape to continue after about fifteen minutes of this.

Sitting close in the jump seat, I eventually convinced him to pull over and allow me to get us home, massive cocaine stash and all.

I had never driven a vehicle in my life, let alone a maxi-van loaded with a thousand pounds of equipment and enough drugs to be a millionaire countless times over.

And so I taught myself at 2:00 a.m, at age fourteen.

I discovered very early on that you do what you gotta do in this life.

DOWN

I learned another important lesson seven years later, on November 7, 1988, at the age of twenty-one, when my father collapsed on the floor before he was eventually found by my kid sister during a bedtime pop-in to see her daddy for a kiss goodnight. He lay in a coma for four days in the hospital and was pronounced dead at forty-six.

The last conversation with my dad was on the weekend before his final attack, while eating Chinese food. On that evening, he wasn't my superior; he was a terrified human trying to calm himself to the truth that he needed open-heart surgery. It was not the routine procedure it is today. There was much more risk involved.

As he spoke to me in our kitchen, the tone of his voice could have said it all. He knew his time on this earth would be very short in the absence of the procedure. Ironically, when he finally was ready to proceed, he never even had the chance.

Fate had made sure of it.

It was over quickly; like that, my path was bound to head in a different direction, and I was hardly ready for it. Are any of us ready when a loved one moves to the other side?

With a history of heart problems, making the statement "it was all so sudden" is probably inaccurate. As a result of his ailing health, it wasn't much of a surprise when you consider it all.

To the best of my ability, I tried to stand in as a father figure (whatever that meant) for a young man. It was probably partly due to sadness for my younger sister and brother and because I was just physically there. But let's be honest here; the job was given to me without preparation or planning. There was zero advanced consideration for becoming their new male role model overnight, as I had not even been clear who I was at the time. It demanded my being somewhat more grown-up, but I hadn't been mature enough.

My older siblings Peter, Tracy, and her husband Peter were there for them, too, as everyone had tried to fill the definitive void left by Dad's passing. Each played a unique role for Elena and Brendan. You could almost say it was a collective goal for us to help fill some part of that parental gap left behind. We helped my mom a lot, but those energies only briefly covered the angst felt when a parent leaves a child so early.

It isn't something I enjoy considering, but my mind is with him for the internal horror he must have felt with his mortality, knowing he was in such poor physical condition. That man, more than anyone, had good reason to be frustrated with **Circumstance.** I often dedicate thought to it without invitation, especially as a parent now.

I think about my dad frequently while also wondering if he would be proud of the man I have become, the man he might have envisioned me to grow into.

One day I might find out.

Ironically, I have already outlived him in age by nine years.

EVE

A rhythmic pulsing of confusion played an encored set within my twenty-one-year-old theater of dismay that autumn. My head was an empty venue, but it filled up rapidly on Nov 7.

I learned what real grief felt like, and it was an unwelcome ushering of critical events. Preferring for this emotion to remain dormant for a few more years, it was simply not to be. My life-long courtship with some darker elements was also set into motion.

Exactly thirty-four years later, I still cherish a card from one very special person received at my lowest point to date. The sender was a young woman named Sherrie. She was an old high school puppy love. At eighteen years old, she once held my heart in a way like no other. We broke up in less than a year; it just wasn't meant to be at the time.

She knew me well; it was almost as though she must have sensed my pain and took the time to comfort it. Her thoughtful intentions, entirely out of the blue, moved me. The impressions her gesture left on me have never been allowed to fade as she holds a special place in my heart for several reasons, even to this day. One of my most recent blogs was inspired by some memories with her from senior year.

Never second guess your caring heart; it needs nurturing. I believe a part of our gifting here is to influence others during their most vulnerable days. As I found out that fall, a little sympathy shown can make a difference in many remarkable ways.

I have learned from her thoughtfulness. My business today is about positively impacting others by helping them through their struggles. This act of kindness paved the way for me to do what I do now.

Experimenting in lightless rooms was how I chose to aggrieve and meet extreme adversity for the very first time. It may have been helpful had there been a book or a therapist handy to guide me. Maybe these could have pointed me in a better direction.

There is no shame in admitting I best provided entertainment by consuming large amounts of drink. Each sip brought on more thoughtfully charged lyrics while listening to some of the most depressing music ever performed or recorded. It was gloriously pitiful.

No one had the right to stop me back then from what I wanted to do. Having never encountered such a jolting event, I did what I had thought might make the most sense. I wallowed in misery for days, weeks, months, and years. Not sure anyone knew how low I had gone, *I* certainly did. It was a dangerous place and joyously was all mine to occupy.

Drinking copious amounts of alcohol didn't work well to ease the emotional bleed, but it sure seemed appropriate to try dealing with things. Each evening after work became a welcome blur of consciousness before sleep. Some nights even sank me further into an utterly dismal array of irrational thinking and behaviors. I'd wake up, head to work, and repeat the drill the next night. It was the most saddening time ever.

Wanting to remain alone, I had also begun to realize a newly found appetite for hopelessness. I gorged myself on it with reckless abandon.

My long-term girlfriend dumped me four weeks after my father passed and three weeks before Christmas — a real class act. She was with me the day Dad died. I felt we had a unique closeness because of it. They say timing is everything; she planned that one out like a pro. Talk about kicking a guy in the happy sac when he is down. She wore a steel-toed boot and attempted a fifty-yard field goal on me.

There was a strong supportive network of friends, but I preferred spending much alone time in this world of extreme pity during the holiday season. Life had resoundingly shown its ugly side, and it had done so dramatically. Who knew vexation could feel so welcoming?

I treasured Sherrie's words as they expressed genuine empathy. I reread them countless times one Saturday in December, a week before Christmas.

The shadow-filled room had been broken slightly by lights draped uncaringly around a small pine tree standing in the corner. Dim holiday colors had persistently been trying to do their job, only to be routinely challenged by certain meaningless songs playing over and over and over on my stereo in the background.

It was all just so perfect.

The drab of nightfall held on to the deafening silence outside. I sat there moping for what seemed to be hours in utter torment. The card stood singularly on the sill next to me. It represented something so much more than words of sympathy scribbled across the top. It was a symbolic reminder to know I wasn't alone if I chose not to be. And . . . it was from my forever-love Sherrie, so it held a ton of weight.

I spent Christmas Eve at my father's icy, frozen headstone. Existing there in the dark and alone with him, I shivered in the raw dead of night at Bayside Cemetery. There was no illumination other than a moon slice shining down to break up the blur of granite rows all around me.

My body hunched over slightly, wanting justification for one of life's arbitrary decisions; I was seeking answers while at the same time wrestling with a certain sense of emptiness. Of all the places I could have been, none other might have been so appropriate for my demeanor as a beer can reacted to my tightly frustrated grip.

There was a feeling of even more sadness within me upon looking down and becoming aware that someone had previously placed a weather-torn wreath upon the base of his freshly inscribed grave. It was probably from another visitor doing the same thing I had been trying to accomplish, but for certainty, the ante had been upped by my pathetic presence there.

The winter elements had taken ownership of much of the ornate red ribbon. The integrity of the wreath was compromised, too, as it had shown signs of fraying all around the edges. The stinging wind constantly blowing for weeks had done a number on it. A wreath was his only present that year, and even then, it was broken.

How appropriate, I thought while looking through the trees toward the lake in the distance, where we used to park our boat on the sandbar and enjoy family swimming time. The reminders of what once was, just kept lining up, presenting themselves accordingly for inspection.

Tragically, I stood on that most sacred evening in December, crying my eyes out to no one. Somehow being forced to accept my younger sister and brother readily would never know the person they would always refer to as their dad.

Having lost him early on in our lives, those two younger siblings became the most significant casualties of his passing away. There, without any notice, a great upheaval was upon them. **Fate** had landed one powerful blow; each learned a harsh lesson as they were only eleven and eight.

There was some resolution for me; at least I'd had enough years with him to remember the time spent and relive the anecdotes of his short storyboard in my mind. Elena and Brendan can never say the same. Their childhood was that of a half-empty upbringing.

Those same two kids on that holiday eve would have to wade through the decades to come independently without receiving any guidance or support from their father.

I remained there for about two hours, still selfishly feeling sorry for my pain. Those two babies had owned the right to do so, not me.

Across Paugus Bay and back home, my fatherless younger siblings had laid down to sleep. Elena and Brendan both dreamt Santa was making his way closer to see them and grant their respective wishes.

Those kids deserved to have eight resplendent hours of peaceful holiday slumber. Even if they were only privileged to escape briefly, from a year, that would become their unwilling nightmare for the other three hundred sixty-four nights to follow. And then, for the remainder of their lives.

Our mother played the elf role alone for the first time. She filled stockings and carefully placed brightly wrapped packages under the tree for each of them. There were fewer presents too because my dad always did most of the buying. He loved Christmas, which is strange because he was an only child. It was not as though he had siblings to play with after opening his gifts.

The following year brought big changes to the Santa department. I did a lot of shopping, wrapping, and stocking-filling for the first time. When the two younger family members still believe, you find a way to divert much of your paycheck toward their cause.

Mom knew when the sun rose on Christmas morning; it would briefly bring a short window of peace before the wake-up call of tomorrow could set back in. I have zero recollection of that Christmas morning. It meant nothing positive to me. I probably got drunk.

Today, I possess knowledge that was a gift from my father that holiday:

No matter how bad you think you have it, someone else has it worse.

Be thankful for your situation always. It might not make sense to do so immediately, but it will become more apparent over time.

On December 24, Peter Alexander Morrison lay at rest, alone and literally beneath me. I stood above him on the snow-covered earth while he forever slept deeper down within the many layers of frozen crust. I chose to visit him. I had to go there. I deserved to be there.

My father, a son, a husband, the patriarch of five kids, was taken from us much too quickly. It was over for him just like that.

He was cold.

Gone.

Thanksgiving sucked, Christmas sucked, and I was confident the new year would represent a definitive step into the unknown without having him there with us.

After that piteous holiday season, I could never truly get back home again.

Silent Night.

Heavenly peace, my ass.

FOREVER

I have always loved music in general; that kinship has never changed, and it never will. Since I was four years old, it has been a part of me. As a musician, I received a drum set in first grade, themed to the Muppets. From there, the seed was planted in my passion soil.

While growing up, there was always a radio playing in the background regardless of where I was in the house, car, or the yard. We knew the words to every song. My dad was a drummer, so some of my talents must have been passed on.

One fond music memory was listening to FM on a favorite yellow Mickey Mouse radio in bed before sleep each night. It was a Christmas present from him one year. To this day, I wonder what happened to that thing. I could accurately tell you the songs I enjoyed hearing, as they still resonate with me in a special way. Micky certainly pulled me along during some pretty bad days.

My fascination with the drums hadn't ended there; piano also captivated me. We used to have an inherited Steinway & Sons baby grand piano in the porch room of our house. There were many days when I sat at that thing, touching the keys, hoping to become talented at playing it.

The song "Music Box Dancer"[1] became a goal of mine to learn one day as I saw myself banging the ivory like a pro when I got older. On Saturday, I even walked down to Greenlaw's Music Store to purchase the sheet music. It then became my long-term focus; music initiatives such as this have always been very serious for me.

On a lighter note, we once hired an older woman to teach me how to play. She had to have been in her early-to mid-seventies. We sat together very closely on the piano bench, so my fingers could be adjusted by her as needed to learn proper placement. Our hips were always touching; we were so tightly perched.

Regretfully, this unfortunate woman had a terrible intestinal situation unbeknownst to any of us when we hired her. Then again, it isn't something you ask when interviewing for a piano teacher. Just my luck, here she was.

I found myself during lessons pressing the keys, trying to make song, all the while she adjusted herself next to me and repeatedly farted through the entire lesson. It was all I could do for a boy who was eleven years old from the onset of the first couple of gassy rips to avoid laughing. It was impossible to pretend I hadn't heard them; the damn bench we were sitting on was vibrating beneath me!

Typically, after about the first seven minutes, it was game over. I broke out in gales of laughter and failed to concentrate again for the remaining twenty-three. This was comedy gold for me. Just too good to let go.

She called it quits after four lessons of this behavior.

There were zero regrets; I couldn't take her regular contribution of rat-a-tooting without bursting out loud. It was simply too great of an ask for a kid my age.

I hadn't signed up for a trombone ensemble anyway.

My short piano career was over before it began, thanks to the "flatulent wonder."

You cannot make this stuff up.

By twenty-two, I had been wrestling with my role in a cruel world for so many years that song appreciation became the only true escape — an opportunity to drift away in lyrics and notes while being gently transported to happier times. It is the only medium I know of that can effectively bring you to another era and place for as long as you choose to remain.

There were a few bands many of my close friends associated my name with back then because I listened to them so frequently. On the surface, one might have thought it a strange obsession, and I completely get that. Maybe too, there were some repetitious tendencies due to my immaturity. Still, I also suffered from obsessive-compulsive disorder, which probably took ownership of a portion of my actions.

People's judgment about this didn't bother me because I knew the true impact and intent behind my affinity for music. If an artist connected in a profoundly moving sense, why not keep going back for another fix? Particularly if it helped reset me back to center.

After thinking long and hard about it, those bands probably saved me, to be honest here. Give me the guitar solo in the live version of "Veteran of the Psychic Wars"[2] on any bad day, and I'll show you a guy who knows how to pick himself back up eight minutes and two seconds later.

Listening to songs provided a harmless escape; they added fuel to my ongoing fire to remain a drummer. In addition to the joy I find in it, music is always my preferred coping mechanism. Even today, regardless of what is going on in life around me, it signifies a uniquely warm light in the window of lost souls welcoming them to recharge for a spell.

Music is also how I have always been able to attach myself to people's memories quite fondly.

For me, when there is emotion, there is a song. As I gaze back upon my time here, if quizzed, I can connect one to every impactful moment I have experienced.

There probably is not a woman I have dated where my mind hasn't automatically been routed to a song as a remembrance of what was, might have been, or was never meant to be. So many songs and so many squandered opportunities for yet unrealized closeness, all because of me.

Some female companions tried to enter my space and remain, but because my brain had been in such an unsettled way, none of them lasted for very long. It was all on me; that aspect of my personality made it very difficult to get close to people.

Love was turned away more times than I could count. It has taken me thirty years to feel comfortable hugging people as a welcome gesture.

Woefully, it was easier for me to get closer to heaven than to another human being. In a way, it still is.

I was just so damaged; lord knows I tried somewhat to find love. My heart has continuously dripped romantic blood; I would not allow it to be shown by opening up. Not for lack of interest, but you obey when your mind convinces you to build a wall after living through challenging experiences.

To those who did offer love, *I am sincerely very sorry.*

I live with those regrets too.

"For Crying Out Loud"[3] is still one of the single most powerfully affecting numbers in my all-time playlist. I would highly suggest if you have never been fortunate to experience this song, do so.

Sit across from someone special, stare into their eyes for the entirety, and allow the lyrics to drain your head from anything else completely. For eight minutes and fifty seconds, your relationship will be in a different place. You can thank me later for this in person at one of my appearances.

Six months after I had turned twenty-four, my favorite drummer and childhood idol, Eric Carr, succumbed suddenly to an extremely rare form of heart cancer. I remember getting a call from my friend Richard telling me Eric had shockingly passed away. He died on the same day as Freddie Mercury, another tremendous talent.

I shook my head in disbelief while standing in the living room with the phone still in my hand, feeling I had again become a playing piece in some cruel irony game. One year and four months earlier, on June 20, 1990, was the last time I had been fortunate to have seen him perform live. Now, the chance to ever meet him was over.

I'd selected my drum set growing up because it resembled one Eric had. The color of the shells was almost identical to that of his stage kit.

Every time I sat my ass down on the drum throne, there again was a quick reminder of yet ANOTHER person taken too soon.

On November 24, 1991, it felt as though the music world had now betrayed me.

THIRD INNING

CASKET

I morphed into THE GREAT PRETENDER while also carrying along some of those unreconciled burdens from my childhood. I toughened up early, not because I wanted to; **circumstance** forced me to do so.

To say I was *living* would not be accurate. To live, periodically, you enjoy and appreciate the beauty and bountiful opportunities around you.

None of this was possible.

I wanted to move on with my life, but I couldn't. The limits of my own confused, directionless, banged-up mind were trapping me.

The immense pain I had felt at my dad's passing was unfamiliar and unyielding. It was my first actual exposure to the unfairness of things in the world. I had seen challenges in many forms but never with anything of that magnitude. Oddly, it was also a veiled preparation for what was to come.

By the age of twenty-six, I had learned much more about affliction and had been exposed to death a lot by then. My existence was constantly walking through some morbid revolving door of "who's next." I frequently struggled emotionally between funerals to make it through an extended period to proceed with what I would classify as having a "normal" state of mind.

The expiring of so many people in my close circles was just supposed to be the follow-through to some unfair plan? The numbers made it hard to accept, however.

How could so many people die in such rapid succession?

All four of my great grandparents, a great aunt, both of my grandfathers, my grandmother, my father, an aunt, a cousin, two very close family friends, an older mentor, my best pal from college, my track coach, two high school friends, the son of a baseball coach, my childhood buddy to suicide, three previous bosses, my weightlifting friend to cancer, his brother in a tragic car crash, half a dozen co-workers, my girlfriend's stepfather, and countless family pets had all been taken away within a relatively short period.

It didn't process well with me on top of all the other stinging trauma which had comprised the previous twenty years.

The continual run of remembrances was one of the hugely impactful personal challenges I wrestled with that decade trying to figure out this thing everyone else kept referring to as our gift.

Why was it being taken away from everybody?

This kind of exposure does a number on an already fragile, immature, and impressionable mind. Thoughts of my untimely demise visited me frequently during these more dramatic days of my twenties. How could I not have been impacted negatively when there was another obituary to read in the local paper and service to attend every time I turned around?

There was even a woman killed at my college. Who was next?

As if earning my stripes on poor employment choices, rationalizing losing friends, family, my idol, and pets had not been enough on my plate, I was also living with ulcers from worrying constantly, ongoing guilt from the predator abuse, a chronic medical condition, relationship trust issues, low self-esteem, zero self-confidence, and had very little faith in a brighter future because of it all.

I was working over forty hours a week in a dead-end job, had no money, paid for myself and went to college full time, drove an embarrassing piece of crap truck, was injured while totaling my motorcycle in a crash, seized the engine in my first car, was a victim of crime, was robbed, lived in a windowless wood-paneled basement with asbestos pipes all around me, enjoyed alcohol, worried incessantly about my younger siblings, and was playing a parental role I hadn't signed up for.

It was a tough lot to face.

Because of being stuck, there was no real joy or anything to appreciate. I had no one to get close to for help. My mind became my ruler and my prison. I was a puppet, nothing more and nothing less.

I attended my fill of regular coping sessions to help me get through those tough times, but not nearly enough. Awful stuff enjoyed tagging along with me; I should have been in therapy full-time, as feeling lost had become the way for me. Sure, I tried taking some meds, but not with any regularity. My stubbornness wouldn't permit me to accept that any were needed at that age. I can only assume there must have been some thought process internally, making me believe I could face any new challenge.

Floundering for years without having an actual plan to get away from the constant swirl of limbo, I certainly never allowed anyone to know my inner struggles. We all do this to some extent. I tried to keep it together inside somehow, without losing all hope for the next tomorrow.

I was in my own dark, locked space without a key — a hidden mind dungeon.

It was my secret.

It may be safe to assume that no one starts at a young age planning to have their first thirty years marred by disadvantage, trial, anger, suffering, loss, distrust, anguish, overwhelm, grief, disability, anxiety, and hopelessness.

Unfortunately, mine had done just that and more.

BURN

The value of money was well instilled in me from a very young age. The concept of building wealth was not unfamiliar. After I lost my dad, I simply was never able to get caught up financially. My mom was supporting Elena and Brendan. I was on my own and trying to help her provide for my siblings in what little ways I could.

Going to college required me to attend full-time and work full-time to pay for it. It was a hectic schedule, but a part of me always remained focused on the bigger picture. I knew one day, my ambitious nature would take me far.

Professionally, I always wanted to get more out of my career than where it had taken me to that point. I had a lousy job, and it bothered me to think that I would be doing the same thing for what amounted to peanuts financially in ten, twenty, or thirty years down the road.

Many of the staff who worked at our company in Portland, Maine fell into that same scenario; none had any financial upside to get themselves to a more stable place. I had been there for a few years and was working around people who had been there for fifteen, twenty, and thirty years who were making less dough and were somehow content.

Why?

We were all financially at the mercy of the local business owner. In no way were we in control of our financial destiny. While it may have been fine for them, I could see my entire bleak existence playing out with every interaction around the water cooler.

I had three business degrees by twenty-seven and wanted more out of my career. Remaining there was nothing that appealed to me but again, the anxiety of the unknown posed a barrier to taking action.

Ironically, my boss became the greatest agent of change for me. His insensitive words seared deep into my head during a painfully disturbing conversation as he stood staring down one winter morning.

This moment became the driving force to pursue my goals and find new employment where I could challenge myself to grow, climb, and attain the levels of success I was capable of. I knew that a change had to be made today, regardless of my anxiety.

"Wearing sneakers, I see," he shook his head, partially laughing. "You are a real genius since it is snowing outside, and we're in the middle of January."

The sneakers he had commented on were the same ones I had been placing wadded-up paper towels and plastic bags in to keep snow water out of the holes in the heels and soles. It never worked, as I sat with soaking wet socks on many days in the winter. Those sneakers were all I had. You tend to make do when you have little.

They were also the same two that cost me a full letter grade in college debate class. I hadn't owned a set of dress shoes either in those days; I presented my argument in filthy worn sneakers, ripped jeans, a Foreigner concert shirt, and no business suit.

"I have no boots; I don't own a pair," humiliated by his arrogant insensitivity.

Ten minutes later, he showed up at my desk again. Now, he had a set of boots in his hand. Walking closer, he placed them on the floor by my chair. They were a pair that his son had been wearing; now, he was offering them to me as if all would be right again.

"I am not a charity case; take them away," I said in a hurt voice.

This took it to an entirely new place for a twenty-something with the lowest self-esteem possible. I had been made to feel almost entirely worthless.

Embarrassed, belittled, and ashamed, I never looked up.

I wasn't sure how with all my anxiety issues and other frustrations, but I also knew I wouldn't allow them to control me anymore. My obstacles were not going to prevent me from reaching the top of my professional goals. That much was for sure.

Enough was enough; embarrassment such as this was the final straw.

I was driven to do something about it.

The one fire which consistently burned bright within me was the knowledge I could succeed professionally and get myself out from under.

Even more so now.

It was on that day I made a personal vow to myself:

- To never treat a human being with such low respect and lack of humility as had been shown to me.
- To consistently reach for more while continually challenging myself.
- To never have my family feel the want for basic necessities.
- To never have to go without as I was doing for years.

Note:

I went that entire winter without owning a jacket. Instead, I only wore one from work while on the clock. There were few long-sleeved shirts to be had either.

My uniforms came home; each had a pair of pants and a long-sleeved shirt. I don't believe I even owned more than two with collars, certainly not any golf shirts. Most of my wardrobe consisted only of concert tees made from a very lightweight material and a few sets of jeans.

START

Mercifully I was ready to make some positive changes by age thirty. Partially it was due to a maturation process, a longing to smile wholly for the first time, and because, too, I knew professionally there was so much more in store for me in this life. The famous sneaker incident drove me to open new doors, that much is for sure. It would take a huge commitment to make some changes, but I was more than ready.

Life had kicked my ass long enough.

I convinced myself there was still plenty of time to capture the perfect future. Sure, there may have been more bad days than good up to that point, but it didn't mean I was forever doomed to repeat the cycle. With a little planning and mapping, happiness more than deserved to come my way. I was also quite tired of being alone.

A distorted expectation had been festering deep in my thoroughly confused mind after having faced so much by then.

It created a belief in being entitled to discover impending happiness from that point on for the rest of my days. The rationale for this was that I had tackled my fair share of difficulties for decades; therefore, the new chapters must only consist of great things in store for me going forward. This only seemed fitting.

Remaining rather old-fashioned, my view on marriage was straightforward. Two people fell in love and then created the perfect life together. Once married, divorce was never in my future. I knew it.

Had we not broken up, I always thought I was going to marry the woman with the steel-toed boots who split my infield that Christmas back in 1988. I never wanted to date, only to be with one person forever.

Some kind of learning curve eventually assists most experiences that come to us. Half of the fun is making sudden shifts in thought to see where the new flow takes you.

My shift came as Stacey Leonard entered my life. I was head over heels and was even the first to say those three magic words each of us longs so dearly to hear at least once in our lifetime.

I said them while we were on my waterbed listening to "If You Needed Somebody."[5] Another life association to a song.

See what I mean?

We tend to be somewhat optimistic regarding our new relationships, family-building concepts, and our overall dreams of securing our forever. This enriches and drives us to take our situation to the next fulfillment level continually. It is a thoroughly healthy approach; lord knows I fell into this way of thinking hook, line, and sinker, needing very much to find something to lift my depressed spirits.

Could it have been possible that the past adverse events may have been the only ones I would face for the rest of my time here?

My dues had been paid early on. Surely the skies were going to become blue very soon!

And they did.

Our union was created on September 18, 1999. We were fortunate to have some initial winds of optimism constantly blowing in our direction. They seemed poised to embrace our collective visage, like a mighty ocean wave rippling through the air. Though you can never see momentum, you always know when it's at your back pushing you along. For us, things had started well.

We viewed the chance of carving out our destiny as a seamless process. It merely required us to engage in whatever actions were necessary to aid in defining its course. We had both subscribed to the idea that the time ahead together is then yours to create and express as you see fit once you get married. You work to make it all possible, and then, magically, new goals begin to surface over time.

Lousy stuff wouldn't happen anymore. It just couldn't. My adversity dance card was already filled forever. The personal shift toward better times was also in full swing by my actions. I was not going to let my anxiety or unreconciled childhood issues control me any longer.

The course of my life needed to be taken back!

We enjoyed the lives of two dreamers who regularly embarked upon each new day together, possessing a great sense of buoyancy along the way. Weekly date nights existed with a cheap bottle of wine and some music, setting the mood quite nicely. Simple gestures and time to strengthen our bond were essential. These were our only days of deliberate romantic interludes, but they lasted consistently for about a year.

Needing more, we moved seven months after marriage, and I became a part of the corporate machine. This is how we ended up in Pennsylvania. Had I stayed in New England, my entire professional existence would have been fraught with regret wondering *what may have been*?

You cannot be afraid to challenge yourself or to keep on reaching. Benchmark your position to others, and then if you find a disparity that is less than acceptable, do something about it. Other than marriage, this was the best decision I had made.

Stacey had just begun applying for jobs; the income thing was all on me until she found one. My work ethic has always been tremendous. I hustled my butt off at the new job and loved every minute. I was making more money than what was coming in back in Maine, but we were down to one income, so it was a wash.

I focused on the potential promotional opportunities to eventually offset this disparity. If you work hard and strive for more, it is important to keep focused on the next job when it becomes available. My new company's career paths were abundant, and I quickly made my aspirations well known. To move up, you needed to play the game. If an opportunity to advance became available in another state, you had to be willing to pack up your family and accept the offer rapidly.

In our first year there, we still struggled mightily. There were days we rolled coins just to put food on the dinner table. It is embarrassing to print that here, but it was the truth. Our budget was tight, and I remained intensely focused on the big picture of climbing that new ladder very quickly to change it. My internal drive was there; it just took some time for everyone to see my capabilities. I was highly motivated to prove I could still become hugely successful despite my learning and processing challenges.

As soon as we settled, we stayed just long enough to get comfortable and then embarked upon the next big thing somewhere else in terms of sightseeing. There were no real restrictions on our time other than caring for our cat, Tubby.

We traveled, enjoyed adult drinks, ate non-healthy foods, laughed a lot, and lived within a new marital structure for the first time. Music was powerful, colors were vivid, and family dreams were attainable. It felt like the spoken words to the song "(Just Like) Starting Over"[5] were written for us.

My only concern was keeping the anxiety in check due to being in a new state, a new job, a new town, a new marriage, and a new corporate office building. There was a lot, but I was determined to cope with it.

My spirit had been reborn!

The new version of Aric had arrived. I desperately wanted to find joy for the first time in my life.

WORDS

It wasn't quite Romeo and Juliette revisited for the modern age, but we were happy for the entire first year of our marriage. To say I was finally in a content place would be an understatement.

It had felt redeeming not to have the constant specter of misfortune hanging above my head as it had done for so long. I was on a positive roll for the very first time ever. It only got better in the fall of 2000.

It's indescribable how the world changes when you receive the news of expecting a child. Our entire purpose begins to evolve immediately and redefine itself. We become more aware of our actions and start to shape our desired parental style. Maybe it is to be sure to yourself; you know what you're doing. It is a feeling which can never be replicated; another one of those instances captured in time along the way is just fantastic.

When it came to having a family, we were a picket fence kind of couple. We already had the house and already had the cat. The only things missing were a dog and two kids! We were certainly going to have children; it was never a question. If needed, I was more than ready to buy a few cans of white paint to complete the imagery.

I got up early in the morning, went down to the parking garage, and greeted Stacey while she opened the trunk for my luggage and then hugged me. Making what seemed to be strange eye contact while biting her bottom lip, she proceeded to hand me an envelope with a note inside. She had never done this before, so I sensed something special.

I don't recall what it said explicitly, but it was just cryptic enough to allow me to read between the lines. She was several weeks pregnant, we were going to be parents. Fenway Park, here we come!

We both had initially agreed that children would not become a part of our immediate family plan unless we were ready to slow down and commit to the change deliberately.

The only problem was that we had not yet done that or planned very well.

So, there we were . . . expecting.

It was all good; who cared.

Growing up with five kids, I always wanted to have children. While being a dad, some of my dreams were doing special things with the kids, like attending a ballgame, teaching them how to ride a bike, going to school events, and having fun around the holidays.

I had looked forward to this from a very young age, probably because I wanted to share some memories in the same way my family had done with me. Now it was finally my turn!

It was going to be excellent for us to be Mom and Dad. We both knew it. Truthfully, we accepted that in addition to being fun and cool parents, we would probably end up spoiling the kids in the process too. But all parents do to some extent. We were bursting with elation from deep within.

As a result of hearing the news, I focused on creating a healthier lifestyle and reprioritizing some career decisions. I never smoked and rarely drank anymore; the possibility of heart problems was always there, thanks to genetics. I wasn't overweight but was not the poster child for good condition either. Seeing my younger siblings go without always haunted me, especially when on the verge of becoming a new dad to our first baby.

One thing was for sure; I never wanted to cause the pain to my loved ones I felt upon losing my father. To be there for your spouse and children for a long, fulfilling run is the responsibility of every parent. I could not imagine leaving this earth without knowing I had done everything possible to remain on it for the benefit of my family.

The thought of Stacey having to raise a newborn alone should I pass away because of my thoughtless behaviors was one I never wanted to come to fruition. Christmas back in '88 at that headstone stung hard. No one else close to me needed to know how it felt. Annually, I do that ritual on Christmas Eve, and it still doesn't feel easier.

We treasured our apparent good fortune of being smiled upon from above in the bigger picture while always remaining true to our shared beliefs. Regardless of anything else in our marriage, children were the most important part of our plan. Boy or girl, it never mattered. The fact that we received such a special present from God was a tremendous honor.

So many families are never blessed with the opportunity to have children; we were very fortunate.

She and I never took that lightly.

One of my obsessive tendencies was to be sure our children would have a large enough catalog of memories of their dad to last them.

Grimly, one Sunday, I calculated a worst-case scenario of minimally how many more years I needed to stay alive for this baby to have enough lasting memories with me. Since I had twenty years with my dad, I figured twenty-five would make for a better catalog.

It sounds morbid, but the previously experienced losses had resonated with me differently than they might have for other people my age.

I came up with the year 2026.

FOURTH INNING

MORE

T hough we resided in a nicer area overall, the crime rate and lack of respect for humanity all around us were significantly eye-popping. I couldn't go three evenings in a row without being woken up by my company's alarm service alerting me to a hold-up, armed robbery, break-in, or violent event within one of the fourteen retail locations I was responsible for. A good night's sleep had never been familiar to me anyway. Like clockwork, you could count on an early morning ring and then either attempt to settle back down or most often remain awake.

I have to believe anyone working for any retail chain there was in fear of violence from customers because you cannot plan for every crazy and drug-fueled interaction at the register. The best you can do in that industry is to try and minimize trouble. Our company did a tremendous job protecting the staff, but there is always increased risk when you have retail sites in some of the worst areas in an inner-city.

I was also afraid when walking across the parking lot in some retail shopping places deep within the hood.

And oh, at many deep inner-city retail store locations regardless of the brand, there are drug deals, hookers in the restrooms, uncapped needles scattered around the curbing, trashcans, and sometimes in the ceiling tiles. It is a risky occasion when you shop in a city. It makes no difference what is being sold inside or who the business is on the sign outside.

I heard the story from one guy at a bar who had a shaking employee toss the keys his way and quit the job on the spot after being held up by a masked man who placed a machete across her throat and threatened to decapitate her in the cooler over a pack of cigarettes. A really nice fellow, making the most of his opportunities in life.

On one occasion in my world, a manager locked the doors to her twenty-four-hour location and quit at 11:00 p.m. on a Saturday, sending me a text message that she had done so.

I spent the night parked at our store lot, sitting in my car watching the entire property get overrun with derelicts defacing my building, destroying my landscaping, doing wheelies on a mini motorcycle, tossing footballs, dealing drugs, guzzling big cans of beer, and shooting up heroin at the front door.

I instructed our answering service to call me every fifteen minutes throughout the entire seven hours until morning arose. Had I not picked up, she was to dispatch the police immediately.

The fear for my survival that night is something I'd rather not experience again. For a guy from New Hampshire, this was something new. Talk about an anxiety attack, dear God. The front seat of my black Ford Taurus became my safety zone in more ways than one.

The crime was everywhere; it somehow still found you when you attempted to mind your own business. The area was like nothing I had seen growing up. Killing each other was rampant in center city; no one was ever safe. What we had always held sacred back home was treated more like a blood sport.

One Friday evening, I was home watching the news as they reported the murder of a woman who'd been shot in the face at point-blank range and died instantly in front of her children while getting into her car at the mall after a family school shopping outing. It stuck with me and became fixed in my brain every time I was in public, either getting out of or walking to my car.

Was I going to be next?

In Laconia, this stuff didn't happen. I had to consider it a part of the deal, knowing there would be one hell of a learning curve, leaving the comfort of a small business and joining the corporate grind.

Since relocating, lots had been going on between getting acclimated to the crime risks, residing in a completely new environment, and expecting a child within six months of getting married. In keeping true to our mission of conquering anything in our path, naturally, we had assumed our first leap into parenthood would arrive with a typical uneventful cadence. There was already enough stress in moving down there.

By mid-Dec of 2000, there had been a slow progression of medical information regarding our baby within the womb.

More and more professionals became entangled in our Morrison family pregnancy web each week. The conversation centered around the baby's lack of growth and development.

The tone and tenor of their words became sharper and pointed as time went on. I always believed the baby would be tiny because Stacey was small in stature; in all actuality, her size had nothing to do with it. There was something else.

The primary issue for most of these reactions occurred after one routine ultra-sound came back, displaying an unforeseen abnormality. Stacey's uterus had never assumed the typical shape of a healthy one. There was a separation from the top middle, creating two separate uterine chambers attached at the bottom. It was formed somewhat like the shape of a heart instead. This malformation was almost like having two conjoined smaller cavities instead of one larger one to create the womb.

The condition is more commonly known as having a bicornate uterus. Growth can become restricted because of the smaller area, and it only has limited exposure to one side. A forming baby never gains the ability to progress within the entire cavity. Despite the restriction, it settles in only half of the space and is still somehow expected to thrive.

Something out of the blue like this changed the entire direction of her prenatal plans.

The bicornate situation necessitated several additional check-ups and visits almost weekly after discovery. It caused all normal planning to swerve midway through and adapt accordingly to how things were going. It was still anyone's guess what was about to surface next.

Unlike many other young people in their early thirties, I was just too inexperienced to understand the complexities of how **fate** works for a married couple.

It isn't wrong to feel giddy about your direction together as newlyweds, but we might have exercised better caution. This is sort of what happened.

Though our eyes might have been slightly blinded from all the initial matrimony stuff, they quickly opened.

Our first baby experience appeared to be more than we had bargained for.

FLOURISH

At thirty-four, I still lacked self-confidence and lived with an off sense of purpose and unworthiness. Those same burdens of self-loathing had followed me since my childhood.

Today I am very confident; back then was grossly different. In those days, I mainly hadn't felt good about being perceived as a role model to any children in any other form except for my ambitious professional drive.

There was always a mismatch in my brain about how I felt internally and how I sought my children to view me. I certainly didn't feel deserving of ever wanting them to be like me or to attempt to replicate his or herself after my career, lifestyle, or persona in general.

While my sense of self had still been very low, I had faith in my ability to work hard and provide for my family. Every job I have ever performed has received the very best effort. When you come from average means, and someone rewards you with a paycheck each week, the value of that simple act becomes a motivator.

Job titles never had much weight; the constant determination and financial reward drove me. There was never any arrogance when I took a role; doing so would have been inconsistent with the guy who didn't like himself. Though these new position names were not important, they remained a bit unsettled in my mind at the same time.

Yea, there was a chip on my shoulder. Overall, one part of me wanted to accept some credit and feel good about myself, but the other wanted to prove I deserved more.

Today I am very thankful; it has driven me continually to keep on trying for new objectives.

Though I had just begun to pursue my career, it had done nothing yet to instill any new inner confidence because I hadn't been able to prove anything from a work perspective; I was still moderate towards how I felt about myself from that point of view.

As a man, on several occasions in the past, I conducted myself inconsistent with that of a positive influence. Drugs, crime, or infidelity have never held a spot, and it was nothing like that. I simply had regrets about some of my previous decisions.

If I hadn't felt the role, I didn't want my children to look up to a father who was fake in trying to be someone he was not. I wasn't ready to be a hero to my children; I knew it.

How can you ever accept your child viewing you as a next-level figurehead when you suffer from low self-esteem?

Someday, maybe my son will take me aside and acknowledge how hard I tried to be the best parent to him. This would be enough and validate my place in this world in some small way.

For a bit of clarity here, some of those words sound like they come from a person suffering from some degree of sadness. Though I was super happy, scattered restrictions from my past visited me all the time. I was in a good place via my marriage, my company was just awesome, but I still wrestled with *myself*.

Funnily, I had not wanted our child to feel like it needed to carry the load of representing the father's name. Individuality is important, and I think a slight sense of identity gets lost by having the same name as your dad. I wanted ours to be different, unique, and memorable.

This opinion is not based upon anything other than my view. Please take no offense to those reading the book if you are named after a parent. My brother Peter was named after my father, so I genuinely have no issue with it. When you write books, you share what you feel.

The whole process of naming was one that we took very seriously. Because of my self-image demons, there was no consideration to do so after me when it came to the first one.

Choosing "Aryn" fit because it was like mine; we could create a unique way for it, and it was relatively uncommon the way we ended up doing so.

Having an unusual spelling, I was sure he would appreciate his too. If you can get through the first day of school each year, the rest is easy. We used four letters like mine, used the letter "A" to begin it, and offered a little twist by inserting a "Y" in there too. Pretty cool spelling we felt.

The derivation of Aryn's middle name came from Stacey's maiden name of Leonard. He is the only one to be able to keep the family legacy alive. We figured with child number two; my middle name would be passed on to continue the legacy on this side.

So there we had it, our firstborn was called Aryn Leonard Morrison! My next hero.

Finally, to clean up this thought and bring this topic to a close.

I support the conviction that children should always aspire to become more successful than those who raised them. It has nothing to do with a name.

Our job as parents is to set them up for future riches by showing them how to become good members of society.

To display compassion and empathy toward those who desperately need it.

And to never believe others deserve to have more simply because they began from a place of privilege.

Encourage your offspring to see everyone as equals regardless of wealth.

Children should reach high to seek greater opportunities than their parents may have been able to realize. Hopefully, some of the various doors that remained closed in our lives will begin to open. Empower them for greatness and then watch them soar.

They should view us as those who helped shape their lives with proper values but not feel like they need to become the people we are.

As long as they are healthy, happy, and ready to fully unwrap their life gift, why care about any other stuff.

In the end, don't we want them to be content with the experiences they create for themselves?

Above all, let them be who they were meant to become in this life.

Isn't it just that simple?

WAIT

I'm sharing many personal details in this book because I believe it is essential for people to understand it is ok to talk about what makes you unique. The good, the frustrating, and everything in between make you who you are today.

As you age, why not release some baggage?

We have all secrets; perhaps by lifting some, finally, you may be able to heal.

You may also want to keep your trials under wraps. It can be embarrassing to let them out; I fully admit that too. Only until comfortable should any of us speak freely about our challenges.

I have done so repeatedly here because anxiety has largely ruled my life, and I have been able to accept it as a massive part of my story. Many people are suffering from it in this world, and my hope in writing this series is to offer comfort to others who also have the same affliction.

When you have a life of managing something so crippling as this illness, the smallest issues can quickly become magnified. My entire time has been somewhat one of avoidance. I know the circumstances which tend to rile me up, so it is rare I place myself in them. As I have aged, it is different now but certainly, it creeps around me.

2001 was the first time in my life when I was not in control of dictating what may happen next, so my triggering went on overload.

I battled it without allowing the condition to completely curb or derail my dreams. With everything around me being unfamiliar, I was triggered daily in Pennsylvania. I fought it, knowing that I needed to keep moving forward with my job, marriage, being a parent, and challenging myself not to let it overtake me as it had once done.

When the weeks went by that February, our pregnancy scenario became a larger mess. One that seemed to build upon itself as our baby distanced further and further from the proper milestone targets. Looking away, wishing, or hoping for things to change would not happen. We were caught right smack dab in the middle of an actual quagmire.

Something else was going on inside the womb that could not be dismissed, which was also theorized to be the other potential reason our baby was not growing.

As it turned out, there was concern our condition might be caused by dwarfism and not as much by the uterus size as initially surmised.

After watching subsequent visual drag and drop examinations on the screen with those white lines, it started to come together too and make sense. The measurements and the supporting information behind this assertion were compelling.

My initial reaction wasn't all that great because there was no previous information about dwarfism other than what little I had already known. I became concerned about the long-term care, disadvantages, and overall implications that came with a person who was born this way. My emotions had nothing to do with the condition itself; it had everything to do with how our roles would change as parents in learning to adapt.

The weird thing was that there was no history of it in either of our families. My dad was adopted, we never really knew about his genetics, so perhaps there was an inherited gene. I'm 6'1, the tallest in my family. It sure as hell hadn't come from me.

We didn't know. So there it was, something new for us to think about in addition to how the bicornate uterus may be affecting this baby.

It is funny; they say things always come in threes. In this case, you could count on us for a triple play. Why the heck not. That's how we rode in the newly formed Morrison family.

Not wanting to be excluded from a trifecta, we rolled along shortly after contemplating the other two areas of developmental hardships into one more juicy bit of wisdom.

A few more weeks after those other conversations had begun to pick up steam, possibility number three was introduced to the party — premature cervical dilation.

This occurs when a baby fails to thrive in the womb. The exact thing ours had been doing for months. Eventually, something will give when this unnatural process continues for too long. When the cervix starts to dilate, it becomes ready to deliver regardless of gestation period.

When this correction happens, the baby's survival comes down to progression and gestation. In theory, if it has developed enough within the womb to support its ability to continue outside of it, there is still a chance. When happening too early, it will not survive. It is a pretty cut and dry thing. The risks dimmish the closer to the due date a mother becomes.

We were far enough out; it was another concern on top of everything else. Because Stacey possibly suffered from it, we had been told several times that delivery might be sudden and without much notice.

We agreed to face this new potential for what it was: another red flag in an already difficult first pregnancy.

At the end of it, there was much to consider. All of those three was a lot to take in.

One morning before driving to work, I sat in the car with a freshly brewed cup of coffee in the holder. It hadn't taken me long after starting the engine to begin wondering what might be in store. If it wasn't one (bicornate uterus), it must be the other (dwarfism).

What was going to happen?

Uterus issue v. dwarfism, nobody could determine with certainty.

How had we found ourselves in such an uncertain place when my perfect future was supposed to be filled with rainbows and pots of gold?

Life sure is an enigma.

VOICE

The worst kinds of dilemma that we had faced before Aryn was conceived was whether to have Chinese food or Italian, wine or beer, and listen to Def Leppard or Aerosmith while enjoying it all.

We had not considered the possibility of becoming parents to a complicated child in any of our advanced planning. Why would you?

Regardless of the outcome, we knew we would have never loved that child less.

There were more obstacles and many more celebrations to come; this was our first series. It was a nudge for the two of us to not lose sight of what had been most important; we were having our first child, and it was all that mattered.

The other aspects of the pregnancy were part of the deal. You sometimes have to employ bigger picture thinking in your life; this was one of those moments.

I believe it is a selfish thought process for expecting parents to inherently feel that their baby must somehow be predestined to arrive without any defects or abnormalities. If found, they automatically consider not wanting to have it anymore or immediately regret their decision to try in the first place.

Many who have lost a child and, as a result, have spent their time grieving, own a unique opinion on this stance. They would give anything for more time, some time, any time.

Having a baby is not a game of chance; it is definitive. There are no do-overs. We step forward and become parents, period. When you commit to creating it, your truest reward begins the day it is born.

To treat a baby as though it were somehow less of a human being due to any imperfection of body or mind is disturbing. I pity anyone who makes decisions from such a warped place.

Feeling as if there is entitlement toward perfection concerning a child is selfish and downright heartbreaking. Those people are living a lie. They should never become parents either.

During six straight months of having these scenario conversations, the baby became more and more restricted within the womb. The not knowing could have done us in, but we wouldn't allow it.

The concerns never went away entirely, but we definitively took stock and reconnected to our good fortune.

It had all come back to our belief in one another that we were going to be ok, regardless of what lay ahead. We eventually agreed that whatever was written for us to happen would happen.

At the center, Stacey and I had wanted nothing more than to be a mom and dad first; ultimately, from there, whatever we got, we got

It was a blessing to have a boy on the way and for both of us to share the experience. We wanted him to be healthy first — who cared about much of anything else?

Dwarfism, low birth weight, deformities, or otherwise, we accepted it.

The fantastic actualization of jointly bringing a new human being into this world still shined brighter over any temporary bumps.

In the big picture of how things are supposed to be, it might have been the plan all along for our first to be born imperfectly perfect to us.

We were not ready to start looking for baseball tickets just yet, but we were finally preparing to become the most lovingly best parents ever.

FIFTH INNING

EARLY

As it was, the domino effect of growth concerns had begun to play itself out entirely by the first week of April. They were at a critical decision-making juncture, as there wasn't any additional time to allow for growth with our baby. He needed to come right out due to significant risk should he remain.

Imagine yourself sitting calmly in an appointment for a check-up, only to be told you will be admitted and deliver the baby within hours.

Aryn was being delivered about six weeks from the due date. It seemed scarily early, but what the heck did I know about it. If his condition were not for the need to bring him out, we wouldn't have been there anyway. Since this cesarean was being performed suddenly and without notice, hanging on for another six weeks wasn't going to happen.

Thankfully, I had already placed myself into a defensive mind in our situation. Getting the call to come quickly to the hospital that day wasn't as wildly stressful as the other three things, but it proved to add a quick layer to our predicament.

Less than two years prior, we'd married, lived close to our hometown, worked for the same businesses, and were comfortably routine. Now, on this afternoon, we were on the verge of having our very first child born sooner than planned, and on top of that, we had no assurances about the current health or physical attributes associated with him.

A positive nugget obtained in all this sudden news was that the development of his most critical organs was far enough to support his survival outside of the womb, which was a great thing to know. While there were always risks, our concerns had already shifted to his physical attributes above anything else.

Today, we were ready to celebrate the delivery of our firstborn. Something many parents are never able to do. Through all of the questions remained this one reality; bringing a life into the world is like nothing comparable; it is also most glorious.

When I entered the room to say hello, Stacey was feeling anxious in the hospital bed. Her concerned facial expressions were immediately noticeable. Apparent discomfort was present too. I wanted to think it was more related to the fact that we hadn't had time to prepare for this to happen so early on, more so than anything of a procedural nature. My assumption was probably very misguided. Abnormalities are still a significant stressor.

She was no longer the young woman who used to go to the Mexican restaurant with me for drinks and appetizers. This morning, she had become a different person. Her demeanor was usually easygoing, but her current aura blew nervousness about the room.

There were only about two hours to gather our thoughts before the delivery, so we attempted to find ways to become somewhat grounded. This sounds good, but there is no way to do it when it's your first.

In the time it took for them to fully prep her with the epidermal and allow me to enter the delivery room for support, whatever meds and sedation Stacey had received were all working well. My millions of pins and needles had returned to stick me; I couldn't stop them. Somehow, they didn't want to be left out of the fun either. Their impact grew by the minute, piercing through the back of my neck and down my spine.

Her desire for more sedation drugs became vocalized as the seriousness of the caesarian became closer. As soon as the long, white curtain pulled down across my wife's midsection, many confused thoughts became intertwined in my mind. I had no idea what to expect. Existing in the moment seemed more profound to me than ever while wrestling to remain calm.

Sitting in a chair positioned near her head, I remained alongside for the duration. If you have never had a child before, a delivery room can influence your psyche. Your mind becomes instantly torn between thinking the absolute best while praying for no complications or surprises. It's an unfair progression, but one I had already prepared for somewhat in advance, thanks to all the tense prior meetings leading up to the day.

The long curtain blocked all visibility from her upper torso to her feet. The only uncovered areas included her head and chest. For the rest of her body, I had zero need to see whatever they were going to do anyway. It had been best remaining a mystery to me. All I cared about was hearing the baby cry for the first time, knowing he was going to be okay.

Not having any idea in advance as to how I might have reacted during the actual birth process, it was hard not to be concerned for my well-being, too, in a self-preservation kind of way while there. Imagine how embarrassing it might have been if I were to become suddenly taken over by a lightheaded spell. Dizziness, followed by a quick trip down to the floor resulting in a goose egg the size of Texas on my forehead, might have been too much. Oh, the shame!

Though we had been fortunate not to have premature dilation, we hadn't received any new information about the status of dwarfism or growth relative to his arms and legs. It was going to be a total surprise.

How do you prepare to see your baby born without proper limbs?

CANDLE

The more we perform a task, the easier it is to repeat it. If you travel the same roads from marker A to marker B, it won't take very long to master driving the route. To the point that we rarely give our actions a second thought, repetition is the key to consistency. In a perfect scenario, this observation makes sense.

When you find out in the morning that you will be sitting in the delivery room awaiting your first child a few hours later, none of us are experts. You have to wing it as best as you know how.

It was good to have Stacey feeling loopy in preparation; she deserved it. If it had been available for me to have a little of what they injected into her, maybe my anxious nerves might have found calm too. Using my voice as a storyteller was merely an attempt to divert her attention away from what was going on beyond the curtain. Even I could tell by the wavering of sentences that the person using this guy's mouth was uneasy.

Neither of us could see a thing, but we heard quick, short, and deliberate commands back and forth from the doctor to the team. There were no planned ideas of how much would be said to her; thinking fast on my feet was the only way to face the time. I spoke reassuringly into her ear as if nothing remarkable was taking place.

She was peacefully drifting in floaty, floaty land while I sat there trying to interview for a job I had no familiarity with—one of becoming a narrator to our past.

The intention was to have her leave the delivery room entirely and take an airlift with me back in time slowly and peacefully to our beautiful wedding day in Meredith, on Lake Winnipesaukee back home. The assumption was that she would relate to my words and embrace the familiar imagery while the birthing process took place behind that mysterious curtain. It reminded me of the time in that old movie about a wizard who remained hidden behind a similar one. In plain sight, you could hear a voice from behind it.

Whatever was flowing freely from my lips was where the distractive story led. I began our flashback process by telling her to visualize a granite bench by the water at the bay. It still sits there, providing a convenient source of respite for tired walkers along the shore's edge.

The same bench in Meredith a few minutes just after midnight on Christmas Eve in 1998, where I had proposed to her by surprise. Every night prior for roughly sixty days, I opened the box, looked at the ring, and pictured my upcoming performance.

Usually, I go back for an hour or so to reflect once a year. There are days I can remain there quietly, and on others, it is just too hard now. My mind justified that it made sense to bring this special time up again. Since she was delivering our first child, the story was a reminder of where we made our marriage engagement official.

On one knee, my leg became wet from the snow. It was a bitterly cold evening. The wind whipped off the water as though pleased by the blanket of shadows that had overtaken the sun forever; it helped rapidly accelerate the proposal process.

In performing the typical ritual of kneeling, it was bad enough to have my lower leg numbing in a snowdrift. Without giving it much-advanced thought, I had also placed the engagement ring on the finger of the wrong hand due to my nervousness. It was the one detail I had never thought about—what hand does the ring go on?

By morning, the newly fallen flakes had erased evidence of two tracks leading to the granite bench. I am sure that those snow prints can still be uniquely tracked straight to our hearts some twenty years later.

Even visible today, if we allow them to be seen, they recount the story of two young, misguided innocents who believed in the power of suggestion rather than of **fate** and **circumstance**.

I am uncertain how far I had taken us in our moment of reflection back to our more innocent days before our first son had been delivered.

Aryn Leonard Morrison was eventually born into our world at 6:10 p.m., weighing in at a whopping 4 lbs, 1 oz.

He was a small one for sure, covered in peach fuzz and a strong desire to get to the hell out of the accommodations where he had been residing uncomfortably for the last eight months. It was his birthday, and all was as it was supposed to have been.

Talk about a weight lifted in that delivery room. They re-confirmed he was a boy, and upon knowing that his limbs all appeared to be proportionate, from there, everything was just frosting on the baby cake. They could have hung a disco ball and played some dancing music there; the party was on!

As usual and customary, the medical professionals whisked him to the NICU to stabilize him and make sure he responded well to this new, spacious, and entirely foreign environment. They took him away so fast that we only had a chance to see him ever so briefly. Aryn initially lived in a warm, incubator-type thing. It wasn't any big alarm considering he had been delivered so early.

His tiny body was having difficulties regulating its temperature during the first few hours, so he remained. His internal organs were developed enough; there were no extreme worries. We never really thought his weight would be a huge factor compared to the limb formation discoveries that had overshadowed the pregnancy.

The sound of your child's first cry simply cannot be given justice in print. I will not even try at this point. Hearing "Peanut" squeak that night remains the loudest and best sound I have ever heard.

Based on his prematurity, he was at minimal risk, and the odds were pretty good. It made sense for him to be there as you mix it all, but it was unfortunate that he was.

At the core of it, we had a son; he was adorable and ours.

Stacey was out of it, and I was just relieved to know he was under medical care from that point. It never even came to me to ask any more questions about his limbs or stature. All was well. As they say, no news is good news. We were both just so happy to be parents; the rest of it became unimportant pretty fast. We took it graciously and thankfully.

Aryn arrived with minimal surprises compared to what had been expected. It could have turned out much worse, but we knew that he would be fine in the bigger picture.

We had been receiving a steady drip, drip, drip of disconcerting information all winter long, and now thankfully, the mystery was revealed. It seemed well worth the unsettling time spent getting there, knowing our first was here and doing fine. He was ours, and we were his.

A rush of positivity arrives when a new life is brought into the world. Not only are the parents afforded a lifetime of unique moments, but they too learn how to appreciate just how remarkable it is to take on a new role. I knew becoming a dad would be the highest point in my life. I could never have predicted in advance when looking down at my boy sound asleep in his warming bed, the new level of yet unrealized love that would immediately be racing through my veins.

Nothing else was more important the day Aryn was born than enjoying him doing what all babies are supposed to be doing.

When you are awarded yours from God, first give thanks, and second, prepare to become an incredible parent.

From there, you will know what to do.

Welcome, son.

ONE

Several weeks passed before either of us had the opportunity even to hold our newest family member. The only contact allowed was via gloves attached to his crib structure. You had to reach through those, and only then could he be touched. There was no skin contact, but at least it was something.

To bring it to some point of reference, prematurity and glove handling were an excellent trade-off for having physical limb deformities. I'd retake this inconvenience any day. The wondering what-if, however, could be done without.

It's never easy to see your child in a hospital room under constant care such as this, but we agreed it was the correct and only option due to his condition. When it is your first kid, it kind of stinks, though; you want to have the ability to hold your baby, look into their eyes, and feel that connection that can only happen by unencumbered human touch. It's a fundamental parental right;

we were denied it for a good reason. He had to remain in that sterile environment and gain strength.

It hadn't been enough to feel tremendous relief that our baby boy had all of his limbs, and had shown the medical professionals they were wrong about him! We never completely dismissed how fortunate we were to have him born without complications, but we certainly had expectations for him to be in our house the next day after his birth.

After just under four weeks, Aryn was making steady progress regulating himself, his lungs were functioning well, and his heart rate was strong. They sent him home in good faith, assuming he would continue on the same course.

The Jeep into the driveway, and I was greeted at the door by our huge, black cat named Tubby. A brand-new baby boy who might take away any attention from him was nothing this cat had bargained for, I am sure. He would not be comfortable sharing space with another person in the house, let alone one of more diminutive stature who too would demand some attention. Most of which had all been paid to him before now. Today his world was changing!

I received the cursory brush against the leg, and then Tubby waddled off to have naptime. It seemed like all this cat did was sleep and shuffle around.

There was a lightly scary air about it. As a new parent, you look inward at the sudden significance of being fully responsible for keeping another person alive. And this one had come home with some minor medical concerns to boot.

It was lovely, but it felt weird too. The child we had known was the one we had been visiting in the hospital. And then, in a funny way, he suddenly became ours to keep.

We placed Aryn into his crib for the first time, changed diapers the first time, and woke him up in the middle of the night for the first time. Everything in this new baby plan was finally completed by having him there with us. It was weird, but only a superb, brief taste of things to come.

Stacey and I had begun taking the roads less traveled as soon as we married. We might have known our good fortune of having Aryn home wasn't going to last for very long.

The first night was as close as possible to having any remote chance at a routine, but it must have been the shortest trip home for a newborn as Aryn took a sudden turn.

Upon the first scheduled visit from our nurse to perform her daily series of tests that next morning, she determined that we needed to rush him back.

His body temperature was dropping to an alarming level, and his heart was suddenly beating irregularly again too. Not surprisingly, he required medical assistance big time. It is hard to imagine what might have happened had there not been a nurse scheduled to be with us each day. Ours was a blessing because, without hesitation, she insisted the hospital make arrangements for his return.

We packed up the car and drove our son across town to live in the hospital yet again for close to another month. He wasn't coming home until he maintained his temperature for an extended period.

Aryn was in his familiar incubator at "New Valley Hospital" within twenty-four hours of leaving it. He was nestled back into his rectangular, sterile box for a second stay. It was the only spot to keep him warm and up to the correct body temperature consistently until he could do so independently. He always slept, so it was peaceful, warm, and perfect for his condition.

Our family dream sat on the shelf for twenty-five more days and nights while waiting for him to improve.

Since we now had our baby, a faster sense of upward mobility became of even greater importance. It also meant doing anything necessary to get there, including traveling, overnights, dinners, events, and a lifestyle not necessarily conducive when your firstborn is in the hospital. But I made it all work.

My retail territory of stores was in Pennsylvania, but our training and offices were in a different state. I spent many more nights in hotels across the borders, proving myself in the corporate world by continually taking on whatever additional opportunities came along.

I remained focused and was on my way to morphing into even more of a hugely driven career-seeking beast. At one point, I was working eighteen-hour days and overnights in the Bronx to help another colleague, then driving back to "Ourtown" in the morning to be with my family.

It was an absolute bitch to take on these extra initiatives, but I knew it would get me some attention. No one was putting forth anything close to this effort.

Something unfortunate is bound to happen when you keep an unbalanced schedule such as this one.

The candle was burning on both ends constantly. I wanted to get back to Pennsylvania to see my son in the hospital, but I also wanted to keep putting the extra time into work to have my name in circulation.

One morning something terrible *did* happen.

Once on the way home from one of these marathon workdays, I was exhausted from being awake for the entire evening on the job. Trouble began as sleep beckoned me in the form of nodding off every so often while driving. Never long, as my head bobbed and then took away the clouds of slumber momentarily.

Eventually, after about 20 minutes in, I fell asleep at the wheel just south of Newark. I was in the third lane on the New Jersey Turnpike, drifting over sideways into other lanes.

I awoke startled by a deafening truck horn that scared the ever-living crap out of me.

But for the grace of God, I had awoken before lane drifting under the semi next to me. Talk about a horror show.

I pulled into the next rest area and had a major anxiety attack. This was closer to death than I had ever been at any other point. It's a much scarier level than when you attend a series of funerals and are exposed to it as a bystander.

I realized then; that my life was not about *me* anymore. It was all about my child.

You can't take stupid risks or make poor choices. When you become a parent, you represent your child's best interest through each of your actions. What I had done was utterly irresponsible, and it might have cost me my life.

Without kids, have right at it and take as many chances with your life as you are comfortable with. As soon as they become a part of yours, it is time for thoughtfulness.

Aryn came dangerously close to being without a dad before they even sent him back home from the hospital again.

Ironically, I almost repeated the cycle of having a child grow up without a father. The very scenario I was obsessed with preventing from happening.

Tubby remained asleep without a care.

TOUR

I will confidently say that you can never prepare in advance for the new love of bringing a child into the world. A ton of responsibility arrives, but what you receive in return makes it gratifying. You will instantly become the most important person to them, as they are to you. If you are reading this book and are the parent of a child, you know exactly what I am talking about here. This type of reciprocal love is absolute gold.

Aside from the work pressures, we were in a great place in just about every other way. Stacey and I enjoyed theme parks and going on the fast rides as much as we permitted each other to eat unhealthy food while walking around those same places. It's just what we did. We had begun to enjoy a great family flow, and a rhythm after our son finally was able to be with us.

Sundays eventually became anointed as our family excursion time in the summer of 2001, visiting many tourist attractions. We created a weekly ritual, traveling throughout Pennsylvania and New Jersey each week while further exploring the area. It was neat to have our little guy in his car seat while we drove around. For many years it had only been Stacey and me. Having a third riding along with us was great. We rightfully felt like a family for the very first time.

Those trips were our way of deliberately investing in each other by having Aryn-time outside of the confines of home. Since we still didn't know many people in the area, we took our free days off seriously by creating family fun together. There were many amusement places in Pennsylvania, more so than we had ever experienced in New Hampshire. Every week, we took out the map and planned accordingly for our next Morrison family experience in the mid-Atlantic region.

From Hershey Park and Bushkill to the Philly Zoo, we drove everywhere and explored as many places as possible. Once, we even drove around New Jersey, winding up over the bridge and arriving at Coney Island. It was July fourth, so we witnessed the eating contests, the aquarium, walked the beach, and took in a few rides.

I had always wanted to go on the famous roller coaster "The Comet" but opted to take a zip through the haunted house instead due to my headache. And yes, of course, we enjoyed a couple of hot dogs. You must go to Nathan's when there; it is somewhat of a crime not to. It would be like stopping by Krispy Kreme and not ordering a doughnut or going to White Castle and ordering chicken.

If you haven't been, Coney Island is just so historic. Make plans to experience it one day. I'll find my way back for a weekend.

Our most frequent road trips were to Knobel's Grove and Dorney Park, the two places we had enjoyed above the rest. Walking around, eating greasy calories, jumping on our favorite rides, and pushing Aryn along with us was perfect. Dorney was on top of our list, so Stacey and I drove over there to jump on the coasters, and people watch on date nights. We had season passes, so our process was efficient to make this happen. After, we enjoyed some wine while listening to many assorted karaoke "characters" attempting to sing at the hotel bar located directly across the street.

Our previous expert level of blind skipping through the first summer months with Aryn abruptly ceased.

There always seemed to be *something* just around the next corner, waiting.

This time, it started with an article of clothing.

SIXTH INNING

GROW

I had found out early on regarding my ability to face many challenges in succession. Way back when, in those childhood and teen years, there was always something getting in the way of enjoying any kind of smooth flow for a long time. Regularly, glancing over my shoulder for the next big thing to shadow me.

When I made that silly reconciliation regarding my future being bright and without any twists or turns, I was ready for the picket fence family and believed it was due to me. Again, all I wanted was to be a father and have a happy family to come home to after work.

As I have spent so many years looking back while composing this series, I guess a colossal mistake made was setting myself up for sudden disappointment every time this sunset-riding plan became more and more distant.

It cannot be clear what I expected in my first two years of marriage, but I know it never included anything, even close to the sudden shock Stacey and I were about to feel a month after Aryn had been home with us.

We had taken the neatest "cool dude" picture of him wearing a blue ball cap while donning sunglasses one Sunday at Hershey Park. It became our favorite to see him wear because his tiny body barely fit in any of the pieces. Somehow, he became a baby trying hard to make it come together for the sake of being adorable.

If anyone walked by us and happened to look down to see our little guy dressed in jeans, wearing a ball cap and sunglasses, I'm pretty sure they forgot if they were having a bad day or not. Wearing that outfit, Aryn made more than a few people smile.

As we continued exploring the area weekly, in less than twenty days, the same blue ball cap was no longer an option for him to wear during our excursions. It wouldn't even squeeze on him tightly. Either the hat was shrinking, or his head was expanding.

We knew the answer to this puzzle. The hat had nothing to do with it. Aryn was deforming in front of our eyes.

An abnormal cranial progression on him had initially been unnoticeable in May and June; by July, it was discernable and became the start of our next fight.

His hairless dome had been getting bigger at an alarming rate. There was nothing subtle about it; the first thing to notice when you glanced down. His enlarging head told a mysterious, silent story. Visually, it was enough to make an average person cower in fear, for an anxious one, this was panic city one thousand times over.

It wasn't just a case of average baby growth. All limbs were proportionate relative to his weight and size. The expansion was significantly different. Its development was alarmingly outpacing the rest of the body. You could see it simply by looking at him.

The same hat he had been wearing so many other days was now sitting upon the top, very lightly perched as a point of reference to our timing. It was now tiny compared to his head.

When you observe one growing large at a steady clip, it doesn't take a genius to conclude that something abnormal is causing it. And unfortunately for Aryn, it probably was not going to be attributed to anything routine or ordinary.

You couldn't look away and think it would get smaller the next time.

It was a problem that was visually getting worse and worse by the week.

TEST

My work territory in Pennsylvania was one of reasonably high profile; it was where a lot of program testing was typically piloted. I had to be on my game due to this unique positioning constantly. For this reason, we had a lot of executives around, so you had to be on your toes. It was a fantastic opportunity to keep my name out there as I was so fortunate to work for a person I connected well with.

It was awkward to head out each day and make casual small talk about our baby. Everyone knew we had had our first child, but no one knew it wasn't quite going as planned. I played the game daily and pretended all was well in our parenting. Without really knowing the cause of his head doing what it was doing, we still had no reason to jump to unwarranted conclusions or share any of it.

Having a child so clearly in trouble became an ongoing coverup for me each time they asked about my new baby boy. It broke my heart talking confidently about how well he was when it had all been just a lie.

No one knew of the constant internal wrestling being refereed within me. Keeping it a secret was the best option, even though it might have been wonderful to sit with a trusted friend or two and allow some of the pressure to release a little.

I kept our baby updates very general to those who inquired and quickly changed the subject. My family hadn't even known about any of the earlier womb drama, and we were not quick to begin opening this one up either.

I wanted to be known for my work accomplishments and not by having a medical history to share. Sympathy was nothing I even remotely was willing to be associated with. As with every other challenge I had faced in my past, I wanted to deal with this new one in my familiar way.

When you start from such a low place of self-esteem, you never want to be in the spotlight. Ironically, this is what I do for a living now!

If I had let on such an unsettling circumstance taking place at home, it was unknown how anyone would have reacted towards me.

Would I not be considered for future opportunities figuring the timing wasn't right?

Was it going to place me into a new and uncomfortable situation instantly?

Aryn's head was big and getting bigger, just like that, without slowing. By the second week in August, it expanded more by the day.

He was in a serious state of medical urgency. If I had to make my thoughts and feelings known, I feared for the worst.

My general conclusion was that because his head had been growing so pronounced in size, there must have been something aggressively dangerous behind it.

I recall going to work and having my free time filled with horrific thoughts about him while putting on the familiar face and acting the happy part for eight hours.

All it took was a baseball hat to usher this next disturbing chapter into motion fully. Once it happened, like a snowball rolling down the hill, so did our newly found cranial expansion begin to gain more and more visual momentum.

Secretly I was preparing to hear that we might have been facing a brain tumor. There weren't a lot of other things medically which came to mind. It was too terrible to entertain aloud and too real to ignore the possibility.

For a guy who loved the game and all it meant, I cursed the damn baseball hat, never wanting to see it again. It represented something else to me, something potentially very sinister.

What happened to it? I have no idea. There is a picture on the wall in the other room with my son wearing the thing. It's all I need to be reminded of that summer.

Some tremendous unknown force had determined that I still needed to be tested further apparently.

Was this all meant for me to gain a form of inner strength I hadn't known of?

Was I to summon it from an untapped place?

Was I being prepared for something else larger for some reason?

I really cannot say.

There was no other way to look at it, while also nothing to do about changing the wind direction. You keep marching into it.

My job was going well; I had found the love of my life and managed to keep some of my anxieties at bay for long stretches. I would never have thought our first baby would open up an entirely new passage for emotional duress.

I mentioned earlier in a previous chapter about the convoluted thought process of falsely believing I had been entitled to having the remainder of my time here void of any additional adversity.

In the summer of 2001, that belief sure as hell was blown to bits. Though I had been tasting positivity briefly upon my lips, the bitterly sour sting of a new adversity canker filled my mouth again.

When I looked down upon our new baby, something foreign was hidden deep within.

So soft, so innocent, and so wrong.

HUSH

I still have a strong appreciation for my co-workers in Pennsylvania; they accepted me quickly after arriving there in this new job. It was an odd time for me, for sure. Being away from home and my son was easier because of these people, and none of them knew my backstory either. Without hesitation, we forged new friendships. To this day, I remain connected with several of them.

Troy, Bill, Marty, Victoria, Sue, Patrick, Sandy, and "Mr. Jingles" - my sincerest thanks to each of you for being there without even knowing what the limited time and interaction with you meant to me.

There were days bonding with you folks when my head was one step away from shutting me down completely. None of you ever knew. Together, we laughed about the random, accomplished much in the workplace, and celebrated our region's successes.

For this, you will always hold a unique place within me.

Of course, as my history has not been great getting close to people, one of these incredible folks is no longer with us. He passed away tragically in a car crash.

Another person in my circle lost to **fate**.

Once again, the grim, hooded bastard had touched someone close to me. He continued to gallop along in the background of my life, waiting to reappear and then offer assurance I should not fear him. I now know you never get away.

You can only hope to be left alone.

What began as sheer excitement and joy with Aryn three months earlier was now more closely related to apprehension and dubiousness. With absolutely zero experience to the contrary, when it came down to the critical struggles of a baby having a deformed head, worrying appeared to be more appropriate than getting shitfaced as I had done when my dad passed away.

The unknown, in this case, made moving on with our mighty plans of being a well-rounded family very challenging, if not impossible. When you consider your newborn facing something like this, it's painful to live it daily and put on the contented-face mask. I did it all the time while being torn up inside.

Portraying an actor was getting old and quite tiring. I continued this performance to keep things hidden and not want any special consideration or treatment.

The summer turned out to be one I would rather forget. It was great with all our family time on those weekends, but it was all overshadowed by questions in the bigger picture. When you watch your child's head getting bigger, there isn't much more any parent wants other than to receive information as fast as possible about the potential cause.

Our support contacts who had once lived close by were now some five hundred miles northeast. Certainly not possible to go out and vent over a beer during times of trial.

There we were, in our new townhouse several states away from friends and family, with no one around to lean on but each other. We still went out to dinner, had date nights, made event plans, and tried to do everything we were supposed to do as the typical married couple.

Alone, navigating through every new twist and turn back then, maybe one could assume this all brought us closer.

We had already been maritally strong. While it sounds nice, it did nothing but force us to jointly say, "Really?"

Reflecting one night at our favorite Italian place just outside the center city my unvoiced concern was that we might have been courting the unthinkable. Many of the words offered by either of us weren't more than a rambling pattern of thoughts, which rarely formed a cohesive sentence. When we did speak, it was about our current situation and trying to make sense of what had transpired so rapidly with our son.

I presented it in these chapters to illustrate how quickly this went south.

All told, it was about six months of constant medical discussions regarding Aryn. Before he was born, and now after.

The candles on the table floated along while providing us an unexpected opportunity to refocus as we attempted to rationalize how our plans together had deviated so much from our initial hopes. We were no longer two young dreamers tempting the universe but a mother and a father who had become victims of chance.

People may have been watching us from across the restaurant that night with envy; I'm sure our "happiness glow" was still there.

The fire was a little dimmer than it once had been. We had coped with so much more at the time than most other newlyweds do. This impacts your radiance.

Fearing deep within my heart that we were suddenly in serious trouble, I downplayed the condition to my wife while we began talking about our next move. Maybe it was easier to play the denial game again than have difficult discussions.

The marriage rainbow bubble was bound to burst.

Other plans for this marriage were in-store, instead of visiting amusement parks and eating hotdogs.

PITCH

My anxiety regularly manifested because of the new medical chapter with Aryn. For the first time, it had been different.

There was a constant need within me to force my stress to be rechanneled. If I was going to be emotionally triggered, this redirection became automatic. I refocused on advocating for my son and not worrying about how I was personally going to let his ailment affect me. Life has learning curves; you become very adaptable when facing significant challenges.

As I mentioned previously, it isn't about you anymore when you have a child. In this case, there was less energy for me to exert stressing, and more focus needed on searching for answers. When you have a baby with a potentially serious medical issue, an entirely new level of grit is required.

Don't waste your energy trying to map your way out of troubled times; you'll go mad. Some will require you to dig deep into your closet of superpowers and become someone else for a short time.

You must put on the big boy or big girl's pants, grow a larger set of balls or breasts, and then get up off the floor.

You will know when it is right.

There are days when we have to dig extra deep — those were indeed some of them.

When encountering your lowest points, you are faced with a choice to either curl up or step up.

How you respond is the next challenge.

When it feels appropriate to summon your fighting spirit, make it happen.

And then walk confidently to the batter's box. The only way to play offense is to take control.

Remaining positive wasn't easy, but you also become a fighter when you become a parent. You protect your child at all costs, and you let nothing stand in your way while you do it.

Our new pursuit for some information was in full gear. The two of us were about to become a force to reckon with.

We wanted answers, and we wanted them now.

SEVENTH INNING

———

FRIES

After faking normalcy for as long as possible, we found out what swimming in deeper waters felt like because we had to. Living in Central Pennsylvania, we were fortunate to be near some of the most accredited medical facilities in the country. We had that in our favor for examination, treatments, and follow-ups. Since the discovery process continued for many weeks, we trekked over to Philly more than ever.

Children's' Hospital became our newest routine destination for analysis, opinion, and long-term care for "Peanut." Thankfully, it was located southeast of us. In our pursuit of answers, the deliberate drive-over became almost commonplace for us every other day. We traveled the route so many times that we knew how to arrive there precisely on time right up to the minute. It sucks to admit it because doing so underscores a tremendous number of meetings that had taken place there, emphasizing the fact that something was very wrong with our child.

A very long drive gives you a chance to worry a lot on the way and again on the return. When you glance over and see your newborn sleeping peacefully in a car seat behind, knowing what you're facing with him could become very heavy is draining. But you remain focused on the end goal to find answers.

Our concern, frustration, and mutual strength grew as his head increased. We navigated through the entire month of August with many testing appointments back and forth down to Philly. It was one hellishly long time without having clarity or even a potential diagnosis.

Aside from the expansion, Aryn seemed perfectly fine and otherwise normal in every other way. By all other accounts, he was, except for the current issue to which we had no clue.

Our lack of a diagnosis was like waiting for one of those firecrackers with a very long lit end to burn. When it is finally going to explode, you can only wait in anticipation.

Somehow, we had almost convinced ourselves on the way over for the long-awaited reveal that it might have been easier to continue to embrace ambiguity rather than know the truth. If you don't listen, it can't be real. Maybe we were correct to assume the worst, and we didn't want to know about it.

The uncertainty *finally* became explained a month later, the first week in September, when the door closed, and our doctor walked in during our appointment.

It was almost a déjà vu encounter. This one took place at a different medical venue and in a room full of unfamiliar people, but its feel was quite similar. Once again, we were destined to participate in a difficult parental conversation.

We sat together as an uneasy couple, trying to remain focused as best as possible while Aryn slept quietly below us. He was comfortable in his stroller, unaware of what his momma and daddy were dealing with. This day was our final reckoning. It was about to get honest, fast.

The lead doctor came across as though he was on a schedule to keep on moving right along to his next meeting.

Frustratingly, I surmised incorrectly that we were nothing more than a quick pop-in to him. He was about to share some life-altering news regarding our child, and his demeanor seemed as if he was running late for an early bird dinner special.

Today was some seriously deep matter for us, and here he lumbered on in seemingly without a care.

This was our *life*; nothing was as it had been supposed to be. Not even for a meeting so important as this one!

Thankfully, he got straight to the point.

I tried to keep my humor to ground myself from the reality of what was happening by creating a cartoon version of this doctor gorging himself on food. It was a casual way to lessen his presence.

He now sat before us, having a juicy cheeseburger, some crispy onion straws, and a chocolate frappe to wash it down while simultaneously sharing his news.

But man, this guy was sharp, informed, and helpful. Cartoon or not, I couldn't have been more wrong about my impression of him.

We didn't enjoy what he told us, but he was first class. Initially, the conversation never gave any consideration to our apprehension. It rolled along with force and deliberation. He undoubtedly displayed much compassion for our situation by eventually yielding to the swelling pain as witnessed through our expressions.

True to our history, Stacey and I listened patiently to some not-so-great news. It isn't any easier to hear people talk about your child having some potentially lousy health issues a second, third, or fourth time.

We only partially absorbed what we were being told. Your mind tends to tune things out when compounded repeatedly with the same negativity.

Aryn had been diagnosed with a condition known as hydrocephalus. His enlarged head was due directly to fluid build-up in his tiny brain.

Rather than try to articulate his condition, I've included the medical definition written by the National Institute of Health. They seem much more qualified to explain his circumstance.

"Hydrocephalus is a rare medical condition with an abnormal cerebrospinal fluid (CSF) accumulation in the brain. This causes increased intracranial pressure inside the skull and may cause progressive enlargement of the head in childhood, potentially causing convulsion, tunnel vision, and mental disability. Estimates report that one to two of every 1000 babies is born with hydrocephalus" [6]

"Hydrocephalus may be present at birth (congenital) or may develop over time due to injury or disease (acquired). Except for hydrocephalus secondary to physical obstruction of CSF passages within the brain or skull by blood or tumor, the exact causes of hydrocephalus are still not well understood.

Babies may be born with hydrocephalus or develop the condition shortly after delivery. In these cases, hydrocephalus may be caused by:

- inherited genetic abnormalities that block the flow of CSF
- developmental disorders such as those associated with birth defects in the brain, spine, or spinal cord
- complications of premature birth such as bleeding within the ventricles
- infection during pregnancy such as rubella that can cause inflammation in the fetal brain tissue"[7]

"This condition is most often treated by surgically inserting a shunt system. The system diverts the flow of CSF from the Central Nervous System to another area of the part where it can be absorbed as part of the normal circulatory process.

One end of the catheter is placed within a ventricle inside the brain or in the CFS outside the spinal cord. The other end is placed within the abdominal cavity but may also be placed at other sites in the body such as a chamber of the heart, or areas around the lung where the CFS can be drained and absorbed."[6]

"If left untreated, Hydrocephalus can be fatal. Early diagnosis and successful treatment improve the chance for a good recovery.

With the benefits of surgery, rehabilitative therapies, and educational interventions, many people with hydrocephalus live relatively everyday lives.

The symptoms of NPH usually get worse over time if the condition is not treated, although some people may experience temporary improvements.

While the success of the treatment with shunts varies from person to person, some people recover almost entirely after treatment and have a good quality of life."[7]

There is no cure for hydrocephalus, but it may be controlled. Thankfully, it was discovered earlier, so there was plenty of time to react, contemplate, and strategize our next moves.

This is some serious stuff; you can't mess with it.

SLICE

Take a few seconds if you have children, and try to apply that very scenario to one of your own. It's tough to visualize.

Think about when you kiss your baby before it goes for surgery, knowing the next time you see them, their head will have experienced something very intrusive, changing them physically forever.

Now, place yourself back into our world. What would you do?

As the doctor calmly talked about this remedy, the graphic image it evoked in my mind contrasted with his words. As it appeared so vividly in my head, a terrible conjuring of this procedure was worth much more than his rambling. The thought of it was horrific. For us to consider placing a medical device inside a baby's head — whether it is a remedy or solution to his condition — was awful.

To cut open the head of a five-month-old is scary, unnatural, and almost barbaric. Skin so pure, untouched, and perfect is never meant to be altered in such a way.

What a disturbing contrast of decisions, if you think about it.

On the one hand, you don't want your child to be cursed by ridicule or continual medical challenges because of this condition and procedure. You wish everything to remain as natural as it can be.

But then, you have no way of knowing what might happen down the road if nothing is done to alleviate the pressure.

It seemed strange to me. Since draining on its own was a slight possibility, why was the head even growing larger up to this point?

If it had an opportunity to do so already, why had it not yet started draining?

Was there a realistic chance it still might?

And who knew what the long-term possibilities would be in terms of constant medical care for a shunt system.

Would it even work on our child correctly per the design?

How many more operations might we be looking at if we decided to move in this direction?

Nothing was clear-cut.

As the meeting was late in the afternoon, after a rapid embrace, we shook our heads, lowered our shoulders, and forged ahead as best as possible. It was a little too complex to figure out immediately anyway, so we simply decided to take a step back, breathe, and regroup for another day.

Almost immediately after being told about the procedure, we knew that it wouldn't be our first option. There was absolutely no way to imagine allowing anyone to perform this procedure on our baby right now.

His mom and dad couldn't do it to him.

While we should only have been worrying about what song to sing to him next, what new toy we were going to spoil him with, or what his first visit to see Elmo would be like at Sesame Place in New Jersey, none of it even became relevant. Instead, we had more medical information to digest — yet again.

In less than two years, I had already worked through a marriage, job change, relocation, single income, bicornate uterus discovery, possible dwarfism, the potential for premature dilation, a near-death experience, a six-week early birth, unregulated body temperature, a heart irregularity, two surgeries, two whole months of hospital fun visiting our baby, and a host of other minor issues.

Today I found out hydrocephalus was the next hurdle placed between us. At the very least, for another year, at most for a lifetime.

SUNSET

The wisdom contained in extreme events sometimes arrives without warning. This was just a depressing, unforgettable day. I remember the insecurity of it all was nuts. Not only was the city in crisis, but the drama was also still unfolding in the skies.

I glanced up after slamming my car door upon hearing on the radio that a plane had gone missing somewhere over Pennsylvania. It was unknown where the aircraft was, but the possibility it might be above us was as real as it got. The entire morning routine morphed into a sudden wave of unpredictability fueled by misinformation.

I recall speaking with Stacey on the phone shortly after arriving to work. There were no TVs around, so my first information came directly from her this numbing autumn morning. She said a plane had just struck the World Trade building in New York, and unrest was rampant in the city.

Like everyone else, I will remember it always. I know exactly where I was standing when my phone vibrated with her news. It shall be etched in my mind, as I was with my boss "William" when it all went down that morning. Together, we ended up back in his hotel in front of the TV. Our minds were numb. It happened to everyone. A death blow ruled the airwaves for hours.

I stood in my driveway and looked up at the sky for the missing plane again. Stacey sat in front of the television with Aryn, watching intently. She had a look of bewilderment on her face when I walked in. Neither of us said much as we stared at the TV for answers.

I reached for our recently diagnosed child and kissed his expanded forehead before placing him in his crib. It was terrible to hear the reports as the world he was born into was spinning out of control.

We elected to do nothing drastic and monitor Aryn's condition and see if it might drain out on its own. The only way for us to know if this scenario was working was for Stacey and me to remain on a rigorous schedule of check-ups over the next year to determine if the growth was slowing down.

Today, his head size no longer mattered, nor did we care about whatever would be thrown our way later. Families were losing loved ones every few seconds. It all seemed utterly trivial, as a distinct thudding sound of bodies smashing through glass became the norm before our eyes on TV.

Our sick baby was safe and warm in the background, not ten feet away. Aryn slept unaware in his crib that the year of his birth would also represent one of the darkest in history. He periodically stirred as the entire world was overheating around us. The only thing of importance was that we were all safe, and we were all together as a family.

The contrast between two compelling forces was beyond words. Empathy versus hate was the message of the day in our house. We spent the remainder together, watching in horror as the delicate balance became so trivial to those who hated us.

As the sun finally set, I took time to stop and consider our good fortune. My reflection was anything but routine or typical. It could only successfully be realized by the compliments of drink. An hour and a half away to our east, New York City was still on fire, and the sky was melting above it. Our country was mourning.

My wine glass and another full bottle of liquid numbing had been waiting to visit me for precisely such an occasion. I washed the slight hint of dust out of a glass and reached for the opener. The next couple of hours were going to be good.

Though I had done a nice job with my stress and coping, the clouds had been circling above me slowly with all the Aryn craziness. I hadn't felt truly and deeply overwhelmed in several years; if there were ever a night to do so, I had picked a good one. Much had taken place there in Pennsylvania; I was long overdue for such an occasion.

Sitting down in the kitchen and pouring the first drink was like spending time with a celebrity. You cautiously approach with good intention, but still, you find yourself hanging around too long. And when it's over, you only remember bits and pieces.

When the first bottle of fun had found a place in front of me, and its contents abandoned, I had plenty of room in my belly for another to pick up where the previous one left off. Neither of us drank much, so having a few extra bottles of wine around made it easy to access supply.

It was a bother to acquire alcohol in that state; you couldn't go and buy it in traditional places like back home in New Hampshire. The Pennsylvania laws were the most screwed-up ones I have ever known. There were no options to purchase beer, wine, or liquor at a convenience store, a package store, a liquor store, a drug store, a grocery, or a superstore; you had to seek out a designated place that held a license, or go to a bar and buy a six-pack over the counter. Adult clubs were BYOB. You paid to enter and then drank the product you carried in under your arm. As said to me by a friend, of course.

The evening was different for a couple of reasons. I didn't consume significant amounts of wine all alone. Good friends flanked me at the kitchen table in unique company.

Two I had known for quite some time but had never been fortunate enough to meet in person until now. I had experiences with them both, often asking questions but getting no responses.

Fate was the first guest to arrive and sit down deliberately at the table to my left.

While taking a few sips of wine, I knew why he had joined me this evening. He had already delivered so many messages in the past. There were many more coming my way, apparently.

He was much more unpredictable in person but felt it necessary to have a few words. You cannot question anything he has to tell you; one can only listen. You don't even have to accept what you're hearing, but you can never change the interpreted context.

He wanted me to know:

Our facing more future adversities would become the new family map to our purpose. He reassured me we had already seen his various workings and had learned multiple methods to adapt to what he brought our way.

This night, he merely wanted reassurance that I understood; our family's journey was never going to be predetermined by the outcome of our adversities.

The decisions we make are independent of the roads we take.

Circumstance was next to arrive, occupying the space to my right.

With a glass in hand, I eagerly welcomed my newest guest to the party, intrigued at what he might also have to offer.

He, too, had something to share, a powerfully sobering thought:

My family might have been on one of those crashed planes filled with precious lives taken from this world too soon, just as so many others were earlier that morning in the buildings.

Those people never had a chance for tomorrow. We still did, regardless of our medical situation with Aryn. We had the opportunity to keep on enjoying our entire lives.

Other families were broken on this night, forever becoming the casualties of evil.

Regardless of what the future held for my family, we were still afforded another day to give thanks.

The victim families of 9-11 could never say that. "Tomorrow" for them was buried beneath tons of rubble, where it remained.

It wasn't difficult to sit there in deep reflection after my two visitors dissolved into the night. I'm sure the wine magnified it somewhat too. It was powerful stuff to consider, but what the hell had some of it meant, and why had it been so important to share it with me on that evening? Was I drunk or going slightly mad? Only time could reveal these answers.

Maybe my two guests expected me to understand more clearly, despite how terrible or difficult the immediate struggles may seem, that if you allow them to be an influential part of your being, then any outcome is still possible when you offer trust and rely on faith.

The day had been a massive reminder for all humanity. My family and I were blessed to be alive and know the sun was coming up in the morning. We needed to create more memories and not focus on the challenges. We had a new baby upstairs just starting. He was a beautiful addition to our union. Sure, he wasn't perfect, but did it matter? No. Nor was it going to matter what other medical ailments might come our way.

Yes, Aryn was struggling, but it suddenly all seemed so minor. We were going to be okay. On the evening of September 11, 2001, on Wild Mint Lane, I just knew it.

My career was in full upward mobility mode, and thankfully we both had great health going for us. I had a loving family to kiss goodnight on that terrible evening. Many people couldn't say that. So, so many people.

Perspective is a curious thing.

For weeks, I watched a visual heartache playing out live behind the glass from one of our offices in New Jersey as the smoke reached the heavens non-stop from Manhattan.

There is no more fabulous gift than your own life. Appreciate it; make a difference in the one you are blessed to have.

And while you're at it, never take anything for granted — even your next breath.

THERE

My initial impression of the corporate world was a nameless, faceless, characterless, non-compassionate, bottom-line-driven, intimidating existence.

An entity who would chew you up, spit you out, and unceremoniously move on to the next sucker. What you gave up in identity to become a part of this machine was then gifted back to you in dollars on a paycheck. This was all fine because it aligned well with the obsession to prove myself.

Another of my ongoing series of flawed assumptions was that we were all just a part of the numbers game whose sole purpose was to add daily profits to the bottom line and often were replaced for a cheaper version of ourselves. I had never assumed that anyone from a publicly-traded company might have compassion for the people working there.

Refreshingly, I couldn't have been any more wrong. I worked with the *best* people and for the *best* organization imaginable.

One conversation with my boss William truly showed a level of understanding which surprised me. Aside from the Sept 11 bonding time together, we hadn't known each other well, as I had only been employed with him for less than two years. We were close to the same age, so I believe he could relate because of that. It is safe to say we were on our way to becoming friends to some extent. Of course, he was still the guy in charge, so the line was there.

Because of the individual, he is, this man had taken it upon himself to follow up with a few more of his supervisors back in our corporate offices. After sharing our medical challenges with some key people, he called to let me know that **all** transportation and **any** medical connections were extended to us to help our son with his medical needs. It was a remarkably generous offer to hear.

I was blown away standing in the Newark terminal before checking my luggage. Other people who hadn't even met me carried a deep concern for doing the right thing.

Here was a classic case.

For much of the bad, some good came our way as well. When the slop hit the fan that summer and fall, my boss and his boss were there for me.

Empathy *does* exist everywhere; sometimes, it just needs to find us when we least expect it. Believe in the positive power of others — karma is real.

The gesture was heartening, and as I learned, this sort of kindness was hardly atypical later on. What a fantastic place I chose to further my career ambitions. Despite my anxiety issues, this communication alone proved that the decision to move away and join this company was the right one.

Since my father's passing, we have all been very close. I am unsure if we always had it in us to be a tight unit or whether his loss somehow worked to bring us together and remain there. When you grew up in the middle of five kids, I guess it makes some sense to think we would stay connected through the years. For support, each person always seems to understand the importance of being there for one another. This level pertains to reveling as well as reaching out to offer a listening ear or an occasional pick-up after falling down.

In November of 2001, I joined my family, which I had not seen in many months, for the graduation of my younger brother, Brendan, from the Naval Academy in Great Lakes, Illinois. It was a very proud exhibition for all of us as we watched the youngest of our five siblings being recognized as a graduate of this esteemed program.

I was resigned to the fact that when, upon my return, there would potentially be some difficult roads ahead. It was a regular thing to reimage my child having such a potentially serious medical condition and how helpless Stacey and I were to the eventual outcome. Though the situation never left my mind while away in Chicago, I did a very good job not allowing my thoughts to become overshadowing.

Before this time, no one in my family had been a part of any conversations regarding Hydrocephalus with me. I always remained closed up to talking about it. The same way I had done since my childhood. This alone says a lot about how private I am.

It was very apparent that they were all extremely worried for Aryn. Everyone displayed a very quiet concern over the weekend. They gave me some space because they were all sensitive to how difficult the times were.

The first day was hazy; on the second, I opened up a bit and shared my concerns in detail. Since we were all together — in the car, having drinks, and back at the bar in the hotel — the elephant in the room needed to be introduced. It was very cathartic for me to talk about it. Before that time, it had remained my ongoing secret with everyone I worked with except my boss.

The days that followed in Illinois needed to be celebratory; I was careful not to allow the medical concerns of my child to become a distraction.

I remember how genuinely upsetting it was; I still never overly displayed my emotions to anyone. It was one of the unhealthiest ways to deal with my concerns. A significant problem exists if you aren't being honest and open around your own family.

Together we cheered proudly as the youngest of this Morrison brood marched by us in uniform and stood at attention.

The only true reality that had become apparent was knowing that we were helpless in altering whatever would come our way in the months to follow.

It was so nice of my boss to call me while I was at the airport the morning of my flight for this family event. It instilled newfound respect in me toward him, not as a leader but as a decent human being. He could have easily not done anything and gone about his business.

He chose not to, and he *did the right thing*. By doing so, perhaps it even softened me a little heading into the weekend.

What a role model he turned out to be. His empathetic call was because of the person and the friend he indeed was. I forever hold him high and the organization high.

Until kindness is extended at the most opportune time, we never realize that simple acts and decisions to comfort others might profoundly impact them more significantly than we expected.

There is not a soul on the earth who hasn't found themselves in the pit of one of life's many disparate misgivings.

Each of us has the ability, with minimal effort, to shine a bit of extra uplifting light in a much-needed direction. All that is required is a sincere desire to help your fellow men and women.

Always keep the batteries charged; you never know when it may be your turn to assist someone with yours.

EIGHTH INNING

DECISION

U p to that point, we had what I would consider a typical marriage. Aside from our sudden and sobering brush with the realities of hydrocephalus, it was normal. Ours could best be characterized as mainly healthy. We had our fair share of arguments over those two years, differing on many world and political views, but none were ever of much substance. It was agreed that she wore the pants, and I had learned to pay for them in many ways.

From a parenting objective, we always wanted to ensure that our child had a similar upbringing to those we had been exposed to in the rural lakes and mountain regions of New Hampshire. In my mind, I sought the best environment for Aryn to grow up in and hopefully replicate those good experiences. The suburb we lived in turned out to not be the place to do so.

First, our property backed up to the interstate, so there was a constant rumble in the background. We couldn't sit in the grass in our yard; it was too loud. I knew these living conditions were less than ideal but hurried to get us settled without ever fully considering the impact it might have on our quality of enjoyment at home. It wasn't New Hampshire with all of that quiet peace we were used to.

The money was great working for this incredible company, so it was a trade-off.

But there was more.

The job was very demanding, and it took up a serious amount of my time, even on the weekends. There were stretches when I hadn't even been able to take a single day off due to short staffing. Our retail store business was not glamorous, but it was lucrative. I was making more money than ever, but it cost much, especially when not being there for my family and keeping a healthy balance.

I received three promotions in two years and became more of a company than a family man because we needed the money severely. My plan to keep on moving up was at full speed. At least that much was going well. It wasn't easy with Aryn being sick.

The final strike for me occurred on December 1, 2001, when my phone rang early in the morning from my store manager "Daniel" calling from "Appleton," Pennsylvania. He was wailing loudly while explaining that one of our employees named "Susan" had been murdered in cold blood behind the counter by a man wearing a black mask.

On the other end of the phone, a grown man was in hysterics as he beckoned for me to get there. He was without control of himself.

A couple of months earlier, Susan had approached me with a request to change her work schedule from the morning to the overnight shift. Apparently, as a single mother to two very young children, she relied on someone else to get them off to school in the morning because she was always working. By asking for a change to the overnight shift, she figured to be out early enough and be home in time to see them off to school. Something she hadn't done in quite some time and so desperately wanted.

It made perfect sense to me, so I granted her request and transferred her to the Appleton location.

In essence, I signed her death certificate.

After calming him down and gathering the facts, I drove to meet him outside in the middle of the night behind the police barricade. The entire front of the lot had been taped off as a crime scene, just like you see in the movies. We were not allowed to go onto the property until midafternoon, some fourteen hours later.

As it turned out, the animal who perpetrated the crime became frustrated when Susan struggled to open the cash drawer.

He yelled at her to "hurry up" and then impatiently shot her through the heart as my other employee "Kim," hid in the cooler and witnessed the entire violent hold-up.

The medics worked on Susan until she died just above us in the helicopter while being airlifted from the location.

The entire murder had been captured on our video cameras, as it was unmistakable where she had taken her last breath.

Kim, who had been hiding in fear, later told me she held Susan's head in her lap, trying to comfort her while her lips turned blue, waiting for emergency services to arrive.

I pray she has been able to live at ease in some way via professional help, but she must have been scarred forever, I know I am.

As the police had finally left the scene, we entered and gaped at the morbid residue. To the left of the front door, a hole in the wall remained where the bullet had exploded a human heart before becoming lodged — the very resting place for the projectile that caused an innocent mom's candle to be snuffed out while merely trying to make a living and provide for her young kids.

This happened because of rage, not money. What an utterly senseless act. It was all over the news, you could not hide from it.

Wearing gloves, using a bloodborne pathogen kit while on my hands and knees, I began cleaning up small red pools, blood splatter, and tiny chunks of human tissue off the floor, counter, and walls.

We spent our time mopping up the remains of a woman who lost her heartbeat for no reason other than that she encountered evil at the wrong time in the wrong place.

You never forget performing a task like that or having one of your staff killed senselessly. It is probably why my company moved me to work in a different state shortly after this incident. To offer me a fresh start and try to cloud the memory of this one. They cared and always did the right thing; I was a mess internally from this.

I know that it rocked a lot of people higher up the ladder than myself. This organization truly stood by its employees for sure. During this event, I discovered an entirely new respect for my boss, what a leader he became, and for the organization.

It had been difficult trying to process the entire tragic nightmare in my home that evening. There is no way to do it effectively; death came swiftly through the doorway without hesitation.

Murder is on an entirely different level when considering the passing of another person. It was disturbing to be so closely connected to another loss.

When you think you're finally able to distance yourself from this horror slowly, it stays with you and draws you back. There has never been any hint of true healing over this.

I kept telling myself, "the money is great, Aric; keep pushing." I knew I also still had to remain grounded and perseverant to get ahead and be considered for that next promotion. "Don't be foolish now."

It hadn't always been easy to do, and I managed it only partially well. My territory required significant professional counseling for weeks after that one. Being a tough guy jackass, I refused it.

A fundamental goal for me back then had been to balance the constant pull between my overwhelm and having medical worries with Aryn. This incident drove me close to the edge by affecting me then, now, and always very deeply in my soul.

The phone call is still heard today, some twenty years later, as it was on that morning.

A thirty-eight-year-old assistant manager took her last breath on **my** payroll. Two very young children woke that morning without a mother because she had been slain on the job while working for **me.**

Two more kids were destined to grow up without a parent, as my young sister and brother were forced to do many years before. It seemed I had become death's bitch, passing on this cursed tradition to another set of innocents.

The pressure and guilt of it all ate me alive, but never to the point that I allowed it to show outwardly. Instead, everything just continued to build up down there in Pennsylvania.

I added this to the constantly growing list of traumatic experiences that needed to be resolved someday. As of April 2022, it still hasn't been.

The dichotomy of life versus death has become an aspect of my perceptions. I wrestle with it in so many ways while still trying to decipher this mortal selection process, knowing I never will be able to.

Someone survives, and another dies; one more chance, and one more final decision.

One more day, one more hearse. One more breath, one more death.

Do we bargain or cross our fingers?

Or do we just . . . wait.

Never trust that which you cannot see.

SCREAM

There was a point in Pennsylvania when things got downright scary at times. What happened in these two chapters was nothing short of hair-raising. Like everything else unexpected that had come our way, these two incidents fell in line next to the others.

If my crazy experiences could be best described through a long series of storyboards, these occurrences took up space on more than a few of them. This was some creepy stuff.

The mysteries of the unknown have fascinated me for as long as I can remember. Share your stories about the supernatural, and you will have an eager listener for hours. It makes no difference if the conversation is about aliens, Bigfoot, or ghosts — I'm all in!

There is no doubt some bizarre things are also part of my story, most of which I will share later in the other three books, but something happened in Pennsylvania that sort of kicked off the series of curious moments.

Our place was an open-air concept. Stacey and I slept downstairs while Aryn did so in his crib up on the next level. Having the ability to hear him upstairs was always foremost in our minds, particularly overnight. We placed a baby monitor by our bed and listened for any signs of distress related to his breathing or newly discovered night terrors.

Not knowing what to expect with his medical stuff, we were overly cautious about staying on top of his actions. He was a restless sleeper anyway, so slumber was not friendly to him.

There was barely an evening when his fussing or crying had not awakened us. Pretty standard most of the time, we assumed; no big deal. His disruptions were all about diaper changes and the need for some bottles, but this all changed in year two.

I always justified the following behavior by thinking his head expansion had something to do with his actions at night. It was never substantiated.

The weirdness started when Aryn was diagnosed with having a condition known as night terrors. I had never heard of these, but know it isn't fun to witness if you are familiar with their effects.

When he had them, it was terrifically unsettling. His demeanor was completely changed. As though he was horror-stricken or even borderline insane. Seeing him this way was like nothing I could have ever believed possible for such a little person.

He would stand up in his crib and lunge at us, swinging his arms wildly. This was hard because there seemed to be no way to calm him; only time could do the trick.

As we got closer to console him, he became more violent toward us. Tears were coming down his cheeks in these episodes, so we wanted to caress him.

Watching a two-year-old toddler looking at you with eyes wide open while thrashing around violently had all the makings of possession.

It was uncanny and out of control to see him like this night after a sleep-deprived night. There was a distinct progression; and no clear way of stopping him once he started.

What a terrible way to be woken up at 3:00 a.m.

There were evenings we could hear him yelling as loud as he could in the middle of the night as if he were feeling something ripping out from within his tiny body.

His eyes were fixed, but the wailing, shrieking and carrying on persisted. Sometimes, he was hugely vocal for over an hour until finally settling down.

My heart went out because he always appeared terrified beyond imagination. As if someone or *something* was inside of him, forcing his tiny limbs to perform unnatural gestures beyond his control.

He even made guttural sounds in between, screaming through the walls.

Was "The White Lady" presented in the next chapter somehow connected to these night terrors?

Was it possible that maybe he'd opened some interdimensional door? And if so, how/why?

What was the reason or purpose?

This craziness continued for an extended period until we eventually moved away, which was long enough. I don't believe he had them after we left. Thankfully.

Aryn never remembered his attacks in the morning. I asked him recently, and there is no recall of them whatsoever.

Thank God, this was some rough stuff.

HER

The other part of this mystery was right up my alley. It added fuel to my ongoing belief system that many of the things we can't explain have some legs. Once again, Aryn was the star.

For a straight year after my dad had passed away, I was cautious about entering the basement living space and possibly seeing his ghost. Upon opening the door, I was always afraid to walk in; he may be standing there looking at me.

The possibility was something I wasn't ready to deal with. It did make some sense, as it was the house he collapsed in just before he died.

The *returning from the grave seed* was once planted in a conversation he had shared with me. If it could prove it possible, he committed to giving me a signal when he passed away.

Of course, neither of us knew how fateful *that* conversation would be a year before his death. Logically, when he died, I feared any signal from beyond may have been in the form of his spirit rather than by some cryptic message left to interpretation. The potential for his reappearance played in my mind regularly after he was gone.

In our townhouse, I revisited the likelihood of it, this time not with the specter of Dad but with a strange woman who mysteriously made her presence known.

A more bewildering scenario unfolded when trying to debrief with Aryn one morning; he voiced to us that "someone" had been visiting in his room at night.

My paranormal antennae were up straight, and I made it a mission to explore this fully. It hadn't felt this was causal to his night terrors because he spoke casually about it over breakfast. Not as if it were any big deal. He enjoyed it.

At first, he did not give much detail and spoke randomly about these visits. Initially, we dismissed the stories ultimately as nothing more than the imaginative babble. But this didn't last for long as the color on his brush began to paint a much more vivid picture.

The mentions of this "visitor" increased with enough frequency for me to begin documenting trends, patterns, and potential causes. Medically, he had fluid building up. We needed to record what it meant if things were getting worse in there, especially when he potentially hallucinated.

Though the dialogue with a toddler just learning to chat tends to be erratic anyway, the continual mention of these occurrences was odd. It is not every day a child comes to his parents and speaks of a nightly "visitor" in his bedroom.

He referred to this person emphatically as "The White Lady" when he mentioned her spending time by his crib. To hear him saying firsthand something potentially unworldly was going on in our homemade tale made it that much more intriguing.

In any case, Aryn regularly told us all about his interactions; it was normal for him to have the encounters two or three times a week. His sharing of these instances increased with such detail and frequency that we had no choice but to hang on to each word and consider what he was saying.

On the surface, it made no sense that someone so young would make up these stories and tell them with such compelling descriptions.

When listening through the baby monitor in his room, it was not out of the ordinary to hear him engaged in banter. There was never a response we could ever hear, but Aryn paused to listen and then replied as though he was chatting away with someone.

It was as if he were having conversations with himself, but he wasn't. He would say things like, "oh, you're silly," or "play with me."

Talk about surreal to hear him like this. I began to think that somehow, he might be in tune with a scenario most of us could not understand.

Neither Stacey nor I knew what to make of the visits. At the same time, she tended to be more skeptical about these types of things. I can say with conviction that we both agreed that a presence was in our townhouse during our time there. It may have been easier to dismiss it, but it hadn't been the right approach for us. This was happening under our roof.

We regularly asked him to tell us about her visits. He was too young to be scared by her, so he thought it was normal. It was fascinating for Stacey and me to hear the details as they unfolded in more unexplainable contexts.

He rattled these stories off like nothing. Neither of us ever made it a big deal for him to talk about it, as encouragement became a part of casual patter. I had never heard of such a thing happening to a toddler.

The real clincher validating something spooky was going on — if nothing had done it for us already—was when Aryn referred to her as his "spirit guide."

When was the last time you heard a toddler use that term?

He didn't make this one up!

We looked at each other when he pulled it out of his two-year-old bag of vocabulary words, indicating that this phrase had been told to him the previous night.

He took it to an entirely new level with this revelation.

Eventually, according to him, the woman claimed her name was "Charlene." It wasn't one he had heard before or repeated from a playground interaction with a little girl by the same one. He had always preferred to call her The White Lady, but he certainly knew her by this name.

Charlene became an almost nightly friend.

If none of it was real, he did a great job of making it seem so. I hadn't doubted any of it.

In addition to her actual name, he described the woman as always wearing a white dress. She was "very bright," which sometimes hurt his eyes to look at her, and was also "very nice."

Aryn "liked it" when she came to see him in his room. Charlene always spoke to him in a very soothing voice.

On several occasions and in a very matter-of-fact sort of way, he recounted to us the varied nature of her visits. She often "floated" up in the corner close to the ceiling or stood by his crib, looking down at him while speaking calmly.

She specifically said, "she was protecting him," while then sharing, "everything was going to be all right."

What the hell did this mean?

One morning, the chills came quickly up and down my neck as he quizzed us on why she said that. Those were the only two sentences he ever repeated fully when it came to his give and take with her. We had no idea what either line meant, other than perhaps a referral to his health?

I have many videos of his telling some of those details. In one instance, in the middle of a chuckle, he mentioned that she had told him to "quiet down," assuming he had been speaking to her too loudly.

While another time, she made him laugh by doing something "silly."

At a different point, we listened as our two-year-old told us she would "enter into his room around the ceiling," and he enjoyed "watching her fly out of his window and play along the treetops outside."

Perhaps even more attractive to note, The White Lady played another critical role in our lives several years later after we relocated back up to NH in the fall of 2004. She made herself mainly known to us on one very creepy occasion, specifically in the spring of 2008 — more on this in the next book.

Could it be possible that there is another dimension to our existence?

One we aren't ever meant to discover or decipher the purpose of?

By slowing down just a bit and questioning reality behind closed eyes, perhaps a new sight will be realized when we eventually reopen them.

Never stop challenging what you think is real; it only takes one breakthrough to validate your effort.

"She" was as present as the still of the night.

PEACE

By 2004, I knew by my own overtaxed mental state that we needed to get back home and no longer exist in fear twenty-four seven. When I felt it, my family had as well. This was not the place to raise a family the way we needed to. There was no question left in my mind. For our safety and my sanity, a change needed to happen soon, or this corporate cat named "Aric with an A" was headed to a terrible place all over again. I could not handle the crime, the traffic, and the travel.

It is scarce that an executive is allowed to return to the same area from which they had originally come. As if my request for leniency had been heard from someone out there in the heavens, I was asked to do just that and relocate back to New Hampshire!

I very graciously obliged. We couldn't pack our bags fast enough at the thought of heading home for another go at family togetherness.

The opportunity was almost a fairytale as I had been resigned to relocating anywhere *other* than New England. It was too good to be true.

Shortly after receiving the news, we searched for a house over a long weekend and eventually purchased it. We moved in September and were busy unpacking for the remainder of the month, and then it started to feel like a home again.

In addition to the various boxes and chaos that arrive when you settle into a new place, perhaps the true validation was that it was our new residence came one morning as Aryn bounced into our bedroom.

Amid performing a cute little happy dance, he said, "Daddy, I'm so glad that Charlene moved with us to our house here. She came to visit me last night in my new bedroom."

And quicker than you can line up for a second helping at an all-you-can-eat buffet in Vegas, we were undoubtedly at our supernatural norm again.

She was back.

There was a weird six-year mirror-effect type thing we had going on. Strangely apparent, we had come around full circle, both literally and figuratively, in 2004. We found ourselves celebrating our sixth anniversary, a job promotion, and had another surprise upon us by year-end.

Compared to previous years, family time had changed significantly in a very positive way. Aryn hadn't shown any progressive signs of hydrocephalus; his condition had thankfully begun fading into the past very slowly.

Fortunately, we had become comfortable doing all the things other families with a young child were able to do. My true family dream was starting to happen, finally.

Work was stressful but financially good to us. Our home was beautiful, set in the woods with a huge front yard, within a very rural and safe area. It cost me more than I had ever thought to be paying for one, but we were ridiculously happy, so the price was all relative.

Aside from Aryn's claim that The White Lady had arrived, we welcomed the brief lull, giving us an excellent opportunity to settle into a much-needed, healthier family routine again.

When you suffer from anxiety, there are days and even weeks when you find yourself almost incapable of moving, thinking, enjoying, or communicating. Before coming back up to New Hampshire, I had been promoted for the fifth time in four years. The previous one had brought me straight into our corporate building and into my own personal anxiety circus.

I recall days sitting in my car trying to calm my nerves, listening to familiar songs. This ritual was repeated every morning for a year and one half before we moved.

Our building was a tallish one; we were on floor eleven, and there were always a lot of very important executives drifting around all the time, ready for bumping into at any moment. This alone was a reason for uneasiness.

Every trip to our offices was a struggle simply trying to gain enough courage to enter the lobby of our building. Once I was in there for a period, all was great with the world. Like back in elementary school, most of the apprehension was short-lived and built up in my head.

Talk about a mind f**k.

Once inside, no one ever knew this secret about me. There was humor, confidence, and professionalism on display. It took a lot for me to do something as simple as a walk to the elevator. I hid it like a pro but was ripped apart on the inside with nerves.

I was vying for continued promotions; eventually, being there was one of those obstacles to overcome. It indeed was a trade-off. I challenged myself continuously like this while remaining focused on the larger family picture to provide for us.

As close to perfection as I might have scripted since we had relocated back to New Hampshire, the need for me to come to the building had all but ended. Annually, I had to be there a few times, but overall, I could put this struggle behind me.

It was awesome!

Financially, we were getting much better, so the money issue had been slowly working itself out. Enough was coming in; Stacey never worked again. She could tend to Aryn and his medical needs.

I was continuing my career pursuits and had become proud of myself professionally as a good provider to my family. It was demanding to have a new position, but my obsession with stability drove the agenda. Even though the lifestyle was seemingly heading in a fantastic direction. Remaining humble and faithful to where I came from never was lost.

Our days together were conducted with a particular carefree spirit once again and always approached by Stacey and Aryn with a smile and an air of playfulness.

We raced at a million miles an hour to go nowhere yet everywhere on family trips. We continually followed a certain loose rhythm, experiencing our family dynamic as a threesome for the first time back in New Hampshire.

We tried our best to start over again in Peterborough as it was great living in the woods and hearing the birds again. The lucky stars seemed to line up nicely for us that year.

In July, Aryn had done time on Santa's lap at one of our favorite family amusement parks, requesting a baby brother. He was serious, and he was genuine. We captured it all on video because it had been such a priceless exchange between the two.

Truthfully, we had discussed having a second child, even becoming a little looser with our birth control efforts on date night. The timing seemed right too. If we were going to have another one — based on our ages, as we were both pushing forty — it needed to happen very soon.

Funnily, his Christmas wish might have been the final catalyst in convincing us to make it happen.

One significant truth we had wrestled before seriously embarking upon a second pregnancy was that after Aryn was born, Stacey should consider having corrective surgery on her uterus if we had planned on another child. It was a procedure we had never followed up on.

Despite Aryn's small birth weight and the hydrocephalus stuff, he was relatively normal in all other aspects of development. To assume another pregnancy might be different, hadn't come to mind. Since her modified uterus already managed to host one baby, it could do so again, restricted space and all. Right?

We planned for a repeat performance in terms of lower birth weight. The chances were good; another one would also be confined like Aryn was. No big deal. Been there, done that.

Our minds had somehow prematurely re-written the plan for a second baby. If Stacey were to get pregnant again, it would be without any new additional risks, despite those involving her already known abnormal condition.

We were already full speed ahead by fall. There was no "if" anymore; this one was coming.

It felt like we had clawed our way back to experience the magic of togetherness as an actual family unit.

What a long strange trip it had been.

NINETH INNING

GLOW

S ometimes, as adults, I feel that if we could harness the optimism that our innocent children possess, our lives would be so much more fulfilled. When life is approached with constant wonder, it is hard to imagine that the little things that routinely bother us can become relevant to our day-to-day lives.

Oh, those priceless observations as told only by a child. Aryn was so excited to tell his baby brother about Santa!

As autumn made way for winter, the holiday season was upon us, and with it, an abundance of gifts for the baby. Aryn was excited with the thought that in one year, Santa would be filling up a stocking and delivering presents under the tree for our new addition as well. He had mentioned to me on one occasion he had felt "the baby may be a bit too shy to meet Santa next Christmas, but maybe in a year or two as it got older, it might feel better about meeting him."

We didn't look back; knowing he was getting his wish of having a younger baby brother or sister was awesome. He delighted in going to school and telling his friends in Kindergarten at Peterborough Elementary that he was going to be a big brother. If any of us were on the moon, he had beaten us to it.

Stacey was as pregnant as possible, and another child's impending arrival into our world made each day much more enjoyable as we headed toward winter of the upcoming new year.

Those initial months progressed without any significant concerns regarding the status of the pregnancy. She had gained the requisite weight that all expectant mothers typically gain during the first trimester without a problem. Stacey followed the standard regimen of tests in those early stages, and by all initial accounts, things appeared to go quite smoothly.

We used much of the seasonal downtime to prepare the spare bedroom, which eventually became the baby's nursery. Located across from Aryn's room at the right of the stairs, we knew he would feel it neat to have it on the same side of the house as his.

We painted it in a soft green color which flowed nicely with the light carpet on the floor. Our spare room had always been a nursery and not a storage space.

If Aryn wanted to "check in" on the baby when he woke up, the plan was to have it be the ultimate trade-off for a few sleepless nights in having him located just across the hall and hearing his brother cry for a bottle. This placement allowed for the convenience of being able to poke his head in at bedtime and say goodnight.

Many presents we received for Christmas filled up the new room, completing the final transformation into a nursery. Stacey did a great job setting it up in detail, creating a unique and warm feel. There was a changing table to the left of the door, the crib on the back wall, a rocking chair to the right, and the room had plenty of light coming in through the two windows which faced the backyard over our deck. It had a certain charm, one representing the essence of a newborn in every way.

We three were marvelously excited for baby number two!

Having it ready so early was ambitious, considering the due date in very late July, but we were motivated to get it done and out of the way. Our new focus was keeping busy in preparation for the delivery.

On New Year's Eve, we revisited a few memories during the night, like when we were just two carefree kids perched on my Suzuki Katana motorcycle and headed over to Hampton Beach for a day of fun in the sun.

We worried about nothing more than gas money and how many dollars were left in my Velcro-sealed wallet to buy us chicken fingers and onion rings for dinner at the Double Decker restaurant in Winnisquam.

Today it is a used car lot.

We relaxed, feeling quite content by the fire in a traditional manner over a glass of champagne and Chinese take-out.

Our white picket fence family plans were back in full swing. We had a new house, a cat, a child and were only one birth away from completing the picture.

AGAIN

If I were a lyrical music writer and needed a project, I probably would rent a place in the woods in January and February up in New Hampshire, light a candle, drink a ton of wine, and weave together some powerfully profound, moving content for a song. If it didn't work, I always have my drums and keyboard to fall back on.

Being pregnant during the winter months of New Hampshire is ideal because unless you're an avid outdoors person who enjoys the snow and cold, there is not much to miss out on in terms of activities.

Truthfully, time almost seems to stand still in the dead of winter here, anyway. The days are short, shadows fall around 4:30 p.m., and the wind can make you feel like you are becoming part of a frozen landscape. You wake up and drive to work in darkness many days, only to return home in the same lack of light eight hours later. It's a rather depressing time.

As the weeks stumbled along that new year, Stacey attended additional meetings with many doctors and medical staff to monitor the status of our baby's growth. Everyone involved was made acutely aware of the first scenario.

We took very few chances, knowing what we knew about her uterus. Truthfully, I went into this second pregnancy without much worry. Knowledge is power.

On February 6, 2006, our doctors focused intently on the AFP (Alpha-fetoprotein) results. The test was part of a series of blood work, commonly performed within the fifteen-to seventeen-week gestation period. This one provides screening for neural tube defects (NTD). The mother's age and ethnicity and these test results can also be used to determine the chances that your unborn baby has a congenital genetic disability.

The only real risk associated with the test itself is that it may turn up a false-positive result, meaning nothing is wrong, and the baby is healthy.

The chance of having a child born with a neural tube defect is one in a half million. The results are given back to you in percentages, which would indicate the likelihood of the baby having each condition.

I cannot recall what it had been with our test, but I know it was abnormally high. Again, no big shock there. It appeared to be the way with both pregnancies of ours. Something always seemed to be going on.

As we found out the first time, jumping to conclusions is not a healthy way of approaching potentially disturbing news. Our AFP results did not reveal any concern for spina bifida or anencephaly anyway. You weather the storm of good and not-so-good information related to any of this stuff.

Before we had too much time to be overly grateful that the first two disorders were not a possibility, one of the display markers indicated the potential for Down syndrome. Stacey's age at the time (thirty-six) and a family history of the genetic disorder were two things that did not work in our favor. I never even knew its prevalence on her side until that day.

This may sound alarming to many families when you hear of a potential condition associated with your baby. We were no different in theory; it was hard to imagine initially. But until you have more clarity, you also worry about something you can't even confirm yet.

With very little professional debate, the only correct course of action was to investigate further like we always had. It meant a lot more was coming our way with probing and diagnostics, but again, we always sought answers from the medical professionals without settling until we had been made aware of all the facts.

This second pregnancy was a weird paradigm, with Down syndrome and not dwarfism like before.

There was a lot to know in preparation should it have proven to be the case. The disorder itself was not much of a problem in acceptance; obviously, it wouldn't change our love for it. As we had felt while facing possible limb formation and dwarfism with Aryn, we just wanted the baby to remain healthy in every other way.

The risk factors were not to be dismissed. We researched the condition and how to adjust for long-term care by having a child born with it. Together, she and I would accept the potential and deal with it.

There were worse things. As we had already found out.

For the most part, upon further discussion, we eventually viewed the possibility of having a child born with Down syndrome as being representative of yet *another* milestone in our marital lives together.

Nothing is guaranteed with a pregnancy or a delivered child. Wrap the unknown deeply within your compassionate spirit. From there, nothing else should matter anyway.

Human life is so much more than what its outer shell comprises. We all possess an energy that flares sincerely from *within*.

Regardless of what is present or not present on the outside, there is undoubtedly a soul waiting to be loved inside. It is all that matters in the bigger picture when you are a parent.

Offer your deepest love and your most powerful hope.

The rest will take care of itself.

FLASH

H ave you ever heard the phrase *"the more things change, the more they stay the same?"*

If you think about the deeper parts of your years to one of the more challenging episodes you have faced, how long did it take for you to be at peace with it?

Were you able to put it away and leave it untouched?

Would it be safe to assume some of the most deeply painful memories are better left where they are and not revisited?

The once unthinkable phone conversation repeated itself while I was sitting at a bar early one evening in Providence, Rhode Island, at my hotel. This gentleman never phoned me after hours, so to see this name show up on my phone, ran a quick flag up the pole.

I hadn't been more than two sips into my chardonnay before listening on the cell to my senior staff person tell me what had just happened.

The flashbacks to Pennsylvania were instant. An absolute tragedy had once again made itself welcome in my region.

I just could not escape **fate.**

The same sick to my stomach, pins, needles, need to go throw up feeling came rushing back.

I placed my wine glass down and noticed the right hand shake while doing so. My head pounded as my heart began beating a panicking new rhythm.

This was the conversation I *never ever* wanted to have again.

Several hundreds of miles to the northeast of the previous shooting, calamity had once again befallen.

The voice behind the words was shaken as the breathing was almost that of a pant.

This person went on to tell me the grim details of a man walking into one of our retail locations, pointing a gun to the head of a twenty-something college student who worked there, and then pulling the trigger.

My employee was packing out the bottom candy shelf just before being killed in cold blood. This individual was simply doing their job.

The police said publically they found a bible in the trunk later on which spoke to the character as being a fine younger person.

Another worker was just murdered on the job.

Yes, I had moved away to hopefully escape from the images of losing my assistant manager three years prior, only to have a new series of death pictures take place under **my** leadership.

There I was, fielding the second call of this nature.

I lost another life.

This all happened inside our store filled with customers at around 6 p.m. It was closed for investigation the entire evening, and the clean-up subsequently took place shortly after.

Just like before. This time, however, there was no motive determined.

The murderer got away and was never caught.

"No one saw anything." It was all over the news.

Most people in my position go their entire careers without encountering anything close to the violence associated with the two killings that took place under my executive sphere.

For some reason, which I do not try to figure out, a couple of young people lost their lives while working in both of the two geographies with which I was in charge. Another lost life.

Late evening and early morning hours emerged as my nemeses. Sleep increasingly became a larger problem for me, even after moving home.

After this second murder, it was worse as I tended to slumber with one eye open, waiting for the next violent crime or alarm call to ring me in the middle of the night.

The only help I could find was in that of a prescription for Ambien. I had already taken it on and off for about seven years; it worked all too well.

As you shake up a carbonated drink with a cap on, it will eventually burst when finally allowed a little room to breathe.

For me, it was a matter of time.

Today, I must live with those realities knowing families lost a loved one while under **my** watch.

Though there was nothing I could have directly done to have prevented either of these incidents from happening, there is an emotional level of accountability with which I have always held myself guilty.

And doing so is excruciating.

CLAP

One little nugget I tucked away from all the medical drama was never more evident leading up to testing. You cannot wake up fearing the worst. It is always best to be strong, optimistic, and positively supportive. The premature conclusions drawn will eat you up before the exams start if you aren't.

A cautious sense of optimism was present toward the follow-up back in Nashua, New Hampshire, but it came with a much-need asterisk. Even the two of us who had learned a lot about coping were still somewhat apprehensive about the results from this next series. It is usually the not-knowing leading up to these events which weigh heavily on a person.

The results, if not great, will manage to tear you apart anyway, even for the most confidently prepared individual. It is a tricky balance; you only win if the information comes back clean. You are at square one with more bad news if it doesn't.

Today was all about the growth markers, so we knew it would be stressful. Evident by our silence within the vehicle, we were mutually uneasy regarding what the upcoming measurements might reveal.

The drive took about forty long minutes. A general sense of anticipation was present in our Jeep Grand Cherokee during the ride over from Peterborough to Nashua. The dirt-filled, snow-lined roadway was the only thing to look in distraction to quell our racing tensions.

We wanted to share the level three-ultrasound experience and view the images of our unborn child for the very first time. We recalled the same day back with Aryn; the photos were ones we enjoyed capturing and bringing home with us and posting on the refrigerator in anticipation of his arrival.

This time, we planned to get the pictures home for him to see his new baby brother or sister when he returned from school. I am unsure if he understood what the images would look like fully. He had no way of knowing they comprised black and white grainy imagery. We forget to mention this tiny detail.

Five other couples were sitting around who were there for exams in the waiting room. To leave and go to the elevators, you must walk out from the medical testing areas and through the waiting room.

There is almost an eerie feel to the floor design because as families are going, they are subject to the glances of all the other people who happen to be sitting there. It is an almost "sizing up" of you and your situation.

Every family I saw passing through the waiting area appeared predictably happy and gratified to have their medical consults. I assumed by the ages of many; that they were experiencing parenthood for the first time. You could see how caught up in the excitement and anticipation of having a baby together they were because it is one of the most special feelings in the world to know you are creating a life.

The facility was bustling as a constant procession of expectant parents made their way to the elevators. To pass the time, I, too, found myself checking people out as they proceeded through the double doors out of the testing rooms, the front desk section, and through the waiting space.

A young couple who appeared visibly distraught walked past the check-out station suddenly. They could not have been much older than twenty-one. This unfortunate little woman had her head buried deep into the young man's chest who escorted her. He was probably the father of her baby; sadly, his face hadn't reflected one of a proud, expectant dad-to-be. It was solemn and expressionless.

As they made their way toward our sitting area, I am sure they thought how terrible it was to walk through this gauntlet of gawkers. They were on display for all of us to know they hadn't been as fortunate as the rest of us.

The room was void of any music; her heavy breathing and rapidly filling nasal passages emphasized their condition.

There was no careful thought given in my estimation as to families like this one. It seems so unfair they are not afforded any discretion toward their privacy in an instance such as this.

It was almost cruel to be forced into the spotlight and visibly allow the world to witness your very personal business. They indeed were not the first family to put on a sympathetic show.

It was apparent to the other people in the waiting area that these two had just received some disturbing information. The woman cried heavily while cautiously taking each step forward to get through our panel of waiting room judges. Her male companion wanted to move past us as fast as possible.

What was going on?

When it comes to your situation, you want the best experience without dealing with anything but the healthy development of your baby.

I wondered what might have been said to them.

This wasn't all just some unscheduled show playing out. Personal elements of their lives were divulged before a group of strangers. I empathized with their struggle, whatever it may have been. Each of us there had immediate sympathy.

How could you not?

It was going on in the middle of a large room where every expectant couple sat patiently on display.

At the same time, the rest were probably thankful that they were not *that* family. I know selfishly, I felt glad it wasn't *us* in there being sized up.

Was she not capable of having children?

Were there some critical medical abnormalities with theirs?

As these two expectant parents might attest, none of us ever know what happens next. Ironically, this day was one they probably didn't want to remember.

Yet, it was one we wanted to capture for Aryn and do just that — remember.

What a strange world.

EXTRA INNING

SHARP

Things moved swiftly during the morning; the schedule went off without significant disruptions. The ultrasound technician spent much time recounting their findings after measuring the length of various bones, a familiar observation.

She explained what a "normal" growth measurement looked like compared to our baby. Her comments were almost identical to those spoken years back during the first one — a real Morrison family rewind.

Again, this one was in the same predicament; nothing was startling. We expected it to happen all along.

She mentioned that the development of his bone structure was minimal and of some concern to her. It was also entirely possible our child might make up for it in the weeks to come.

Unsurprisingly it was still somewhat rough to hear again because you immediately begin to have similar doubts.

Was this going to be a repeat?

Would this baby do better or worse in the womb?

Should we automatically plan for it to be delivered early?

So many questions; the point of being there was for some answers!

The sex was apparent; we looked at the screen together and knew. During our viewing of the remarkable first images in ultrasound, it was in short order confirmed we were going to have another boy. Aryn was finally going to get his wish. Something he wanted more than anything in the world — to have a new baby brother.

Much additional time was used analyzing the baby and making various casual comments regarding his progress. In doing so, our specialist also noticed something curious midway through.

When compiling all the bone structure data, she guided us via the white arrow toward a thickening dark spot on the back of his neck. Pointing it out, neither of us could even see it. She insisted it was there, a marking indicative of the potential for Down syndrome.

Based on all the other information, we had complied about our possibility for it; it made our decision for the next test suddenly *more than appropriate.*

Amniocentesis is a procedure where a small needle is inserted through the mother's abdomen to collect a sample of the amniotic fluid. It is a test to determine if there are chromosomal disorders in the fetus.

As with any procedure, there are always risks associated. The needle can cause harm when the ultrasound is not carefully performed. Premature labor may be induced suddenly because of infection too. And if all of this isn't enough to think about, the placenta could be ruptured by accident, bleeding, fluid loss, and a few more unpleasant possibilities can happen.

I have included here some additional information to add context:

"Complications of amniocentesis include preterm labor and delivery, respiratory distress, postural deformities, chorioamnionitis, fetal trauma, and alloimmunization of the mother (rhesus disease).

Studies from the 1970s originally estimated the risk of amniocentesis-related miscarriage at around 1 in 200 (0.5%). Three more recent studies from 2005-2006 estimated the procedure-related pregnancy loss at 0.6-0.86%. A more recent study (2006) has indicated this may be much lower, perhaps as low as 1 in 1,600 (0.06%)." [8]

We reasoned that the benefits of knowing more about what we were dealing with far outweighed any potential complications during the procedure. The odds of anything happening were so low that it wasn't worth a millisecond of our time to decide on proceeding forward to have it done. We were already there, so getting answers to our questions was the point of the day anyway.

The results took up to fourteen days to return, but at least we could put it behind us. I thought we would get them right back, to hear this blew.

All the others had gone smoothly, so the day had become a complete prenatal success in general.

Again, we were fortunate to have another baby. If there were additional complications, we were better prepared than most due to our history with Aryn.

The thought of having a needle stuck into an abdomen is an unpleasant one, no matter how you explain it. I was happy it wasn't my stomach facing the pointed end of that thing in the next few minutes. They said it was like the feeling associated with getting an ear pierced, but it sounded terrible to have it done. God bless my wife; her tolerance was always high, but this one seemed challenging to think about. I chose not to be present during the insertion and waited behind the curtain in the same room. There was no reason for my being in there to see it happen.

The doctor did the test efficiently; she probably had done hundreds in her career, if not thousands. She was very precise, and it didn't even take very long. Stacey complained shortly after about tenderness, but that was to be expected. Have someone stick a sharp object into *you* and see how pleasant it feels. Thankfully, according to her, it was not as dramatic as we had thought.

We exited the facility with ultrasound pictures in hand and great relief, knowing all the testing had finally concluded.

Somehow, when you see those pictures, pregnancy is truly authentic. You cannot manufacture love when you lay eyes on your child within the womb for the first time. It is beyond fantastic to experience. We knew that Aryn would be so excited to see these images of his new brother.

All was good in my life when we left the facility that day, very good.

TWO

fter leaving that last medical appointment, it was still relatively early, so lunch at a local chain restaurant made sense for our carefree agenda. We brought the new ultrasound picture of our baby boy in and briefly discussed the meeting we had just come from. Stacey was in good spirits despite having a needle pierced into her belly. It can probably be attributed somewhat to the knowledge that she and I would be new parents again. It felt great.

We may have confused the entire restaurant that afternoon as our reveling only lasted about fifteen minutes before we put on a dramatic performance for the unlucky lunch crowd. It was impromptu and completely unscripted — sort of like when a person begins to choke during their meal. The entire restaurant eventually becomes silent as everyone then takes notice.

No sooner had we ordered than all normalcy surrounding such an everyday experience unraveled for our planned lunch date. The innocent, little celebration and reflection time ended abruptly as

Stacey very starkly returned from a brief visit to the ladies' room with a look of utter concern.

She walked to our table without blinking; her eyes were piercingly staring through me. The anguishing and painful facial expressions represented the likes I had never seen in my previous ten years. She turned pale before me and began shaking like someone wearing a soaking wet shirt with no jacket outside in Minnesota during February.

I barely recognized the person standing there. She had somehow switched places with the woman who had gone into the restroom not five minutes prior. The stranger had kidnapped my wife and meant business.

In what was almost one fluid motion, Stacey grabbed her jacket and purse and then headed toward the door while finally making a statement to me, "I think something is wrong; we need to leave right now." She stood there agonizing, pale, hunched over, waiting at the threshold in obvious distress.

I knew she was in considerable discomfort below from how she was carrying herself, bent, clutching her stomach. Our visual act was some dire stuff playing out for all restaurant-goers to witness over their liquid lunches in the bar section too. No one knew what the hell she was doing. Neither did I.

The waitress asked about taking the meal with us; the food had just arrived. I immediately requested the check, emphasizing that we needed to leave this instant; there was zero time to discuss what we hadn't yet eaten. Our server stared at me as I threw down a bunch of money without waiting for change and got my wife out of there.

We hurriedly walked across the frozen snow and ice-filled parking lot toward our Jeep Grand Cherokee. Holding Stacey's arm, we shuffled slowly around to the passenger side. I could feel her trembling forearm inside her sleeve as she hyperventilated. She was so upset that she had not even been able to tell me precisely what was going on. It felt like we were in a race against time, yet I had no idea why.

I hadn't known if Stacey had slipped on the floor or was having labor pains. Something terrible was going down, and we needed to return to the same medical facility in Nashua as quickly as possible. That much was clear.

The only information she shared between the random sobs and short breaths was that "she had just lost a significant amount of fluid."

I completely froze up when she said this. For a pregnant woman, I knew this was never good.

What did it mean?

The parking lot was full of snow, the footsteps were quite deliberate in moving around as safely as possible without slipping and falling. I hurried around the back of the vehicle to reach the driver's side. Coming from the rear toward the door, I happened to look down at my feet just before grabbing the handle to let myself in. Under it was an area about a foot wide, void of any snow or ice. This was the only spot around my car with bare pavement. It was weird to see it without any prominent winter elements. Snow and ice had taken over the ground there, but not in this one spot.

As my eyes glazed ever so briefly, I noticed there happened to be two pennies. While I typically am not overly superstitious, I bent over and picked them up without giving them much thought. They both showed heads up, a customary sign of good luck. I placed them into the righthand back pocket of my jeans on a whim.

The flashers were on as I drove back to Dartmouth Hitchcock while posing as a NASCAR driver with a sick passenger beside me. The white hash marks on the highway almost became one as we sped back for help hauling ass down that highway, doing everything possible to minimize our time. Though it was only a ten-minute drive, it seemed to take much longer. Surprisingly, I didn't get pulled over.

Stacey was on the cellphone to them, recounting what had occurred in that ladies' room just a short time ago. Listening to her words made me feel both sick and terrified, swirling around in my gut at the same time. Nothing sounded very positive at all.

I could faintly hear them on the other end, telling her to get back as soon as possible. After hanging up, she repeated "oh my god, oh my god, oh my god" under her breath, just loud enough for me to make out her words.

The standard pins and needles were back, immediately pressing against my spine, head, and neck. I knew they would triumphantly return eventually, not that soon after the last inducing event. These new conditions were just right for them to stick into me again for a while.

The hospital indicated they would be outside with a wheelchair waiting for our arrival. When turning in a few minutes later, I knew something more was up immediately. The number of people standing there under the awning at the entrance made quite a fateful statement.

They carefully placed my ailing wife into it and rushed her back to the facility through the front toward the awaiting open-door elevator. There was no time to waste; they knew it, too, based on their hurried march.

After finding a parking space in the lot and running into the building, my blood was racing as though I had just completed a marathon. Not even looking at another person below, I proceeded upstairs to the floor where the medical staff examined my wife.

The damn stage-like waiting area had suddenly made it known that I was the next guest to perform. Stacey and the team had wheeled on by them from the elevators to the examining rooms before I sat down.

Without seeing a single set of eyes, I could feel them all watching me. They, too, were wondering what was happening. A wave of absolute helplessness overcame me while sitting there, waiting for the next surprise.

If someone had asked me how to spell my name, I would not have been able.

The same uplifting day, which had made our becoming parents again so special, was instantly bringing us swiftly and without warning to a terrible and yet another foreboding place.

DANCE

When I was a little boy, Christmas, baseball, and music were the three kings of my world. When some days were bad growing up, my escape was always to bring back memories associated with the holiday season or baseball. Music then set the audio backdrop to my visual mappings. I wouldn't say it was a direct form of escapism, but a way to always try and use happier memories to change my attitude.

As we age, the ways to cope become more mature. When you have a system of calm that works, it makes all the difference between a complete shutdown and an ability to keep moving forward. Sitting there offered me the unwanted time to race through some methods I might use to remain semi-relaxed. Somehow, I needed to refocus my energies and stay grounded for what was coming.

Perhaps there was not even a good reason to prepare? Maybe all was going to work out ok, and this was an overreaction in my way.

251

For now, there was too much confusion mucking up any attempt to relax. I tried, but this was next-level pressure. I couldn't make it happen.

Quietly sitting alone in a waiting room full of strangers, completely unaware of what is happening to your wife and child, your mind races. Minutes, seconds, and chunks of time become grouped. Songs play at random without being selected, never to be heard in their entirety before the next one interrupts. Lyrics stick briefly without making any sense as to why they are stepping into the bigger picture of the moment.

No one told me if the baby was in trouble, if Stacey had a heart attack, or if another internal health scare was taking place between the two. The quick actions taken by the staff as we arrived emphasized the severity of *something* going on.

Awkwardly one of my employees phoned me as I sat there going through this quizzical state. "Brent" wanted me to revel in his financial success for the previous month based on his territory's business profit and loss statements. As he spoke, my world was shattering apart without him ever knowing.

I exhibited the confident Rockstar tone and congratulated him as I typically would any other month. My voice was calm and undistracted. I was the boss, the role model, the epitome of assurances. It was my job to do so as the company man I had become.

Just another typical workday for my team.

Their leader was a mess inside and coming apart by the second. Thankfully I had evolved into an expert at hiding my emotions, so it was no big stretch to pretend. Business as usual. While two hours away from the office, I was swallowing gulps of uncertainty over and over in succession.

Two round pieces of zinc and copper held hands in the right backside pocket of my pants while I prayed for some kind of impulsive luck to drip onto my skin when I touched them. Irrationally I believed in their magic. Those coins somehow found their way to me; it was not by chance. Maybe my old friend **circumstance** had paid me another visit.

My racing thoughts lasted approximately twenty minutes but waiting felt like an hour. The only thing to do was sit nervously, watching my bouncing right foot.

I looked like a tap dancer with the toe-end of his shoe superglued to the floor. Only my heel came up and down while the rest remained still. This nervous action continued as if my leg had been battery-powered and turned up to the fastest speed possible.

After tapping about three hundred times, a nurse came and led me through the last door on the left down the hall. Hesitantly, I walked toward it as my breathing increased in pace with each step closer.

The room was empty except for Stacey, the doctor treating her, and two nurses flanking each side. It seemed some hidden communication had been underway before my entering because no sooner had I sat down than a procession of medical staff marched into the room.

Here I had thought my life had been trending into such a positive new direction, not five years after getting married; it was reeling all over again.

The date was exactly one week after Valentine's Day. It was February 21st, 2006. Not a single person spoke a word.

END

The space had filled up, as we had somehow become
instantly very important people. I recognized two of
them, Doctor "K" and Doctor "B." Everyone else could
have all looked the same.

There was noticeably too much pressure in the room. It felt like
when you force more air into a balloon, knowing it will explode at
any moment. This helped create one of the strangest
environments I have ever been in.

Of course, it featured the two of us.

It was a small room packed with all those people. Silence
shouldn't have been foreign when cramming so many into one
area. The only discernible sound was rubber sticking to the floor
with each step from the soles of shoes worn by our medical guests
moving about to find seats. Squish and squeak, squish and squeak
was all I had been in tune with.

Stacey had already received some disturbing news and was partially aware of the screenplay which was about to be presented. I grabbed her hand while tracing the ceiling vents with my eyes for any distraction to keep me focused.

Not much earlier, we were celebratory while looking at the picture of our unborn son. We were now about to engage in what appeared to be a critical discussion. It felt as though my world was going to fall apart like so many other times before, at any second.

Not again, more tough news? What the heck was happening? Just spill it!

Our doctor spoke very factually and empathetically regarding the significant fluid loss and subsequent extreme cramping. He continued; there had been reason to assume the needle from the amniocentesis test had potentially caused a rupture in the placenta. While Stacey was in the bathroom at the restaurant, it released suddenly.

He paused and allowed us to let it all sink in.

Truthfully, I hadn't an idea what this meant. Was I to have been reading between the lines here for some big picture innuendo?

My already bewildered mind did not allow me to comprehend what was being presented fully just then. This conversation was at a level I had not yet been exposed to.

After pausing to look at us, I am sure he could tell by my unmoved facial expression that the information wasn't registering correctly.

Then changing his presentation style rather quickly, he did anything but beat around the bush, speak in riddles, or try to soften the sad details which followed.

He was adamant; things were not looking good for our baby.

After dismissing all those threats of potential trouble before the amniocentesis procedure, they now meant something stark to us.

Had the risks so clearly explained beforehand just now become our most recent worst dream?

Were we instantly becoming a statistic, defying the odds in the worst ways?

Was our baby the one in sixteen hundred this happened to?

Had this all been caused by the amniocentesis test?

Or was it an entirely different issue altogether, like premature cervical dilation?

Bryan Cowan, MD, reported to Parents Magazine in its article on common miscarriage causes that "Uterine anomalies account for about 10 percent of miscarriages."[8]

"A weakened or incompetent cervix is a problem that can lead to miscarriage because toward the end of the first trimester; the fetus has grown large enough that the cervix starts to bulge. If the cervix is weakened, it can't hold the fetus in."[9]

Was our situation a result of her bicornate uterus?

Cleary, our baby, was not very big. What the heck was going on?

I remember thinking, *This can't be right*, while repeatedly shaking my head slowly back and forth.

The entire travesty had taken place faster than an episode of *Columbo*[10] on television.

Without a word, Stacey looked over to me before I had an opportunity to say anything of comfort to her. Two tear-drenched eyes spoke only of blindsided heartache. They had done their job of articulating silent speech for both of us.

We could only, expect . . . Our baby was not going to survive.

Acting as the anointed puppet to the all too familiar cloaked man of finality as always, this time he was nearer to me than ever before.

Close enough to whisper in my ear —

"Hello Again."

POSTGAME

US

Though we never talked about it casually or in detail immediately after, we both knew the situation when we left Nashua. The next aspect of our lost baby horror was the unsettling fragment of how and when it would end officially. I am unsure how any conversation would begin, flow, or end when you are bantering about such a heavy consignment.

Maybe Charlene was sent to us to take care of him when it happened? There had to be a reason she was brought into our family. This was the only one that made sense.

The pictures we saved for Aryn to see of his new baby brother were still sticking out slightly from the top of her bag on the floor in our vehicle. It hadn't seemed appropriate even to take them out and give a sympathetic look at my son before heading home.

There he was in print, a life full of promise never to be gifted to any of us.

Part of me wanted to; the other just knew I couldn't do it.

Laying eyes on an unborn soul who, not ten minutes earlier, we were told was going to potentially pass away, seemed a cruel thing to do.

Maybe another time, maybe never.

There was not any conversation within the car during the ride home either. The drive amounted to us knowing we were headed toward a state of *waiting*, with no immediate plan other than to anticipate something horrific to happen soon.

While sorting through all the unanswered questions and subsequent prayers, I thought about us having to share some tender words with Aryn regarding his brother when we got home. It would be challenging for him to comprehend at the age of five if he could even understand it.

I'd reminded him in the morning on the way to school that we were coming home later with a picture of the baby. He'd jumped from the car enthusiastically and ran in to tell his teacher the exciting news. He couldn't wait.

Tonight, I envisioned him sitting on the couch wearing his PJs, drinking out of his milk cup with the curly straw, waiting to see what Mom and Dad had to show him while sitting with his legs hanging, bouncing up and down so innocently.

He was too young to understand at this age that this talk would be the most meaningful discussion we would ever have with him during our entire lives.

Instead of sharing the most treasured conversation with him, his parents would have to tell him about the uncertainties of **circumstance** and **fate** for the first time.

I doubted much of it would flow with a single tear when the conversation came. Death doesn't register for young kids, nor should it. But we still had to tell him. If he broke down, we hadn't even planned what to say.

I pictured my son in a matter-of-fact way, reaching his tiny hand over and grabbing a chip off his snack plate calmly while we began to speak. The food selection might hold as much weight to him as our words, but who knew?

I assumed Aryn might listen to what we offered as nothing more than just words and block from his mind the fundamental nature of what was being said. Or maybe this was just my way of forcing my mind to shelter him.

For a child his age, the sun always rises, and the birds always sing. A face with a smile must accompany every crayon drawing of a person or animal on a piece of paper.

The Easter Bunny comes every year, and heaven is a far-away place where Grampy rocks in a rocker and looks down on him while Aryn's former cat Tubby sits quietly in his lap.

There is no suffering, and bad things always turn out well. All are just so pure in young eyes. As we get older, we lose this sense of clarity.

Circumstance becomes an entirely different concept to digest.

I didn't know how to effectively explain in a way any five-year-old could understand that he was not going to become a big brother.

How do you communicate to your only child that the room he helped prepare for his eventual arrival would never be welcomed by the sounds of baby giggles within its walls?

How were we all going to deal with the truth day after day, knowing the nursery room just outside our bedrooms was to become nothing more than a symbolic reminder of how precious our time here is.

We were going home to explain to Aryn; that he would never hold the baby, even if only for a day. Never hear him cry, laugh, or even see him smile.

None of us would ever know what his voice would sound like or what color his beautiful little eyes and hair might have been.

Fate had stepped in.

We had to explain to Aryn that his new baby brother would be born asleep, not wake up or even open his eyes.

They would never share the same pillow, look for clovers, explore the woods, share stories, or play ball in the front yard.

Instead, we were going to have to explain to Aryn that Santa could not grant his most special request; his baby brother would soon live with God rather than with us and fly free with the angels.

Somehow, we would have to find a way to make sense of it all ourselves.

Just not on this day.

UNTITLED

I will Alway*S* *lo*ve, <u>YOU</u>.

265

AFTERWORD

When you compose a series of books based on your own life, it requires a lot of profound discovery back as far as can be remembered. If you take the time to dissect your days truly, the lessons learned become apparent. Most of us don't immediately understand them; it seems somehow they mature over time and only then become much more readable.

I believe in sharing; when acquiring wisdom through the years, it is appropriate to examine our lessons at the end of each milestone.

When I got married, I enjoyed having the ability to dream again. My flaw was to see things only as I assumed they might be. There is a mistake in doing this. It can become easy to exist as someone with amiss priorities via a skewed perception of how things are *supposed* to be rather than how they *will* be.

Fulfillment doesn't always work the way we hope it might; the deviation is a part of our time here — plan for sudden unforeseen changes to your days.

Life is not scripted, no matter how much we might believe we can make it be.

Always set realistic expectations and accept things will change anyway. You will save yourself some frustration if you try to keep a somewhat even keel with your ambitions.

From there, stay the course.

The real question with a life story such as this one is where exactly (aside from death) the telling of each segment ends.

For me, this seemed to be an appropriate place to do so.

REFERENCES

1. Frank Mills. "Music Box Dancer." *Music Box Dancer*. Polydor Records Ltd., 1979. Album.
2. Blue Oyster Cult. "Veteran of The Psychic Wars". *Extra-Terrestrial Live*. Columbia Records,1981. Album, CD.
3. Meatloaf. "For Crying Out Loud." *Bat Out of Hell*. Cleveland International Records (Epic),1977. Album.
4. John Lennon. "Starting Over." *Double Fantasy*. Geffen Records,1980. CD
5. Bad Company. "If You Needed Somebody." *Holy Water*. Atco, 1990. CD
6. National Institute of Neurological Disorders and Stroke, National Institute of Health, Hydrocephalus Fact Sheet, and Publication Date NIH Publication No. 08-0385.
7. "Hydrocephalus Fact Sheet", NINDS, Publication Date April 2020. NIH Publication No.20-NS-385.
8. Andrea Dashiell and Chaunie Brusie, RN, BSN Updated October 1, 2020, Parents Magazine.

9. https:/InfertilityTexas.com/blog/What-You-Need-To-Know-About-Miscarriage-And-Pregnancy-Loss/

10. *Columbo*. Created by Richard Levinson and Willam Link, Universal Network Television, 1968-2003.

ACKNOWLEDGMENTS

The wonderful people below will never understand the full knowledge of what they offered me in terms of strength to carry on.

You don't need to.

Those who are listed impacted me in some meaningful way during this period of my life. My gesture here is small; your efforts deserved to be recognized because they were so big.

And if you don't see yours, there are more books in this series with many more names listed.

I wish to express my "sincerest thanks" to every one of you.

Helen, Bob, Elaine, Tracy, Peter, Andy, Lisa M, Elena, Brendan, Paul B, Thomas, Peter A, Corban, Chloe, Mary-Beth, Daniel, Marvin Lee, Albert, Petey, Julie A, Steven G, Zanny, Sherrie L, Chris G, Greg I, April M, Eric S, Jim S, Cheryl P, Pam O, Rachael L, Mike L (RIP), Roger O, Laura G, Troy H, Patrick H, Don R, Will W, Manny B, Blanche, Bill D, Danielle, Cindy B, Debra J, Mike B, Scott C, James T, Brian and Chrissy L, Cliff B, "Oilcan", Paul A, Bill C, Jim B, Spencer T, Mr.P, Scott M, Adam, Jo, Andy H, Dean R, Joe B, Dr.K, Kathleen, Karen, Jeff B, Joy A, Dawn E, Lynn B, Josh E, Stacey A, Haley G, Heather S, Teddi B, Paige B, Kathy A, Victoria I, RK Smith, Ewe, Ralph P, Todd L, Jon D, Doug C, Dan G, Honest Bob, Sidney A,

Francis H, Susan K, Tim R, Greg H, Junior, John D, Amy D, Randy P, Alan S, Lisa L, Kathleen C, John M, Rick A, Sue G, Jody S,Paul B, Kate C, Cedric, Steven O, Jeff A, Marty K, Brian B, Roman O, Vinnie S, Scott S, Winnie W, Julie P, Rene L, Charlie I, Sandy B, Wally M, Fat Joe, Pete M, Warren M, Jeff B, Bret E. Boy, Barb Z, Tom V, John L, Ron B, William S, Irene B, Diane C, Heather S, Cindy C, Sandra A,Dennis M, Martha J, Glenn D, Peter T, Stacey S, Jennifer V, Armando S, Roland S, Tim D, Chris G, Linda M, William E, John G, Paula P, Nate M, Adam O, Harry S, Andrea M, Bradley S, Patrick A, Don B, and the entire ADVERSITY ROCKSTAR family.

ABOUT THE AUTHOR

Aric H. Morrison studied at Plymouth State University, graduating with three business degrees and a minor in mathematics. His education has always been the foundation for all the continued success in the business world that he has been so fortunate to achieve.

He is a business executive with over thirty years of experience in corporate settings. Aric has always held a passion for leading and developing people at every level of their professional careers. Today he uses his life experiences to help others facing some of their most challenging moments in life.

Aric H. is an inspirational speaker, an award-winning author, an international writer, and a multimedia personality. He is the founder of Adversity Rockstar LLC. A business where he uses his platform to inspire, motivate, and change lives via his stage speaking, writing, blogs, books, podcast, and frequent co-host radio appearances.

Mr. Morrison is the author of five and has plans to continue writing a series of twelve new self-improvement books in the foreseeable future. Most of which have already been written.

One of his most ambitious plans is to have fifty books published in the next ten years.

To date, Mr. Morrison has been seen on TV in over one hundred thirty countries, his blogs are read in over twenty-five, his podcast is listened to in over a dozen, and today he speaks on stages everywhere!

COMING SOON :

MORE FROM THE STEALING HOME SERIES

POSTSCRIPT

One of my obvious intentions here was to make sure you could become familiar with each of us who make up this Morrison family. To better understand our trials, I wanted you to become a household member by the end of this first book.

It was important for the readers to feel they had become a part of our journey. Almost as if they, too, were walking along in the shadows with us.

Opening myself up to the entire universe here in *Heavenly Peace, My Ass,* was not easy. The mission of helping others was always why I shared this story.

The good this book can offer to someone who may be feeling low in their place far outweighs the almost insurmountable effort it took to see it come to fruition.

Understand that you are not alone. Everyone faces difficult roads along the way from birthday to birthday.

By now, if I have accomplished my mission, you have become a part of my family.

Consider reading the next release in this series. It will take you on another leg of the continuous journey that has defined my place in this world.

If my story ended with this book, I would be content to have shared it in this way. And then my life would have turned out much differently.

We don't get choices in our destiny; we get the wind at our backs, and the ability to explore. Then too it shifts and blows directly at you. I understand now when this happens you *must* still continue to walk forward.

What we discover from there internally, is solely up to each of us.

It is the beauty of our time here.

Rest assured that the **Stealing Home** continuation will force you to do some soul searching. *Heavenly Peace, My Ass* was only the beginning.

Welcome to the family.

FINAL

Authors work ridiculously long hours and take tremendous pride in their craft. Many of us have forfeited much of our lives to deliver meaningful work. I take special effort to create a written piece that fully represents what flows from my head to my keys.

We don't punch a clock or work regular schedules. The hands of a writer are full accountability. If the job isn't done, they keep moving until the fingers call it quits.

This is what we do.

If the project doesn't feel right, I don't force it. When you read my blogs, books, or articles, hopefully, you know by now they all come from a special place.

Any support you may feel appropriate to give by leaving a positive review is much appreciated. It can go a long way for an author—so simple a task, but often not performed. It only takes a few minutes but can make the difference with book rankings.

Please share your impressions with a friend and suggest they read my books. It all helps tremendously for folks like me to continue to reach more people via my efforts.

It is why I do what I do for countless hours every year.

And . . . the next time someone asks if you've read any good books lately, hopefully, you now know how to respond!

Thank you for placing yourself into my realm, if ever so briefly. It means the world to me.

Truly.

Keep smiling; life is wonderful.

Cheers . . . A

Made in United States
North Haven, CT
15 May 2022

19194996R00163